Reviving Democracy

Citizens at the Heart of Governance

BARRY KNIGHT, HOPE CHIGUDU
AND RAJESH TANDON

EARTHSCAN

Earthscan Publications Limited
London • Sterling, VA

First published in the UK and USA in 2002 by
Earthscan Publications Ltd

ISBN: 1 85383 884 5 paperback
       1 85383 881 0 hardback

Typesetting by PCS Mapping & DTP, Newcastle upon Tyne
Printed and bound by Creative Print and Design (Wales), Ebbw Vale
Cover design by Danny Gillespie

For a full list of publications please contact:

Earthscan Publications Ltd
120 Pentonville Road
London, N1 9JN, UK
Tel: +44 (0)20 7278 0433
Fax: +44 (0)20 7278 1142
Email: earthinfo@earthscan.co.uk
http://www.earthscan.co.uk

22883 Quicksilver Drive, Sterling, VA 20166–2012, USA

A catalogue record for this book is available from the British Library
Library of Congress Cataloging-in-Publication Data

Knight, Barry, 1947–.
    Reviving democracy : citizens at the heart of governance / Barry
  Knight, Hope Chigudu and Rajesh Tandon.
       p.cm.
    Includes bibliographical referrences (p.) and index.
    ISBN 1-85383-881-0 (cloth) — ISBN 1-85383-884-5 (pbk.)
    1. Civil society. 2. Political participation. I. Chigudu, Hope
  Bagyendera. II. Tandon, Rajesh. III. title

JC337.K65 2002
300--dc21

                                                      2001006719

Earthscan is an editorially independent subsidiary of Kogan Page Ltd and
publishes in association with WWF-UK and the International Institute for
Environment and Development

Contents

List of Illustrations

About the Authors

Barry Knight, based in the UK, is a social scientist who in the past has worked for Cambridge University and the Home Office. Currently, he is Secretary to Centris, an organization that pursues innovative social policy and practice. He is also advising the UK government, the British Council, and the Charles Stewart Mott Foundation on policies towards civil society. Barry works with the Centre for Voluntary Action Studies at the University of Ulster and the Centre for Civil Society at the London School of Economics (LSE). He has written seven books and has published more than 75 articles. Barry is responsible for evaluation in the Commonwealth Foundation Citizens and Governance Programme.

Hope Chigudu, based in Zimbabwe, is a gender specialist who co-created the Zimbabwe Women's Resource Centre. As well as being a grassroots activist, Hope has advised national governments and worked for the United Nations. In her work, Hope specializes in strategies for organizational development and change. She has published widely on gender and civil society development. Hope is the African member of the Commonwealth Foundation Citizens and Governance Programme team.

Rajesh Tandon, based in India, is one of the world's leading authorities on participatory research, civil society and democratic governance. The founder of the Society for Participatory Research in Asia (PRIA) in Delhi, Rajesh holds a number of important international positions, having been Chair of CIVICUS. Rajesh is involved with the Johns Hopkins Cross National Project on the

Third Sector and is leading the Indian component of Sussex University's Institute of Development Studies Governance Programme. He is the convenor of the Commonwealth Foundation Citizens and Governance Programme.

Foreword

Graça Machel is one of Africa's most prominent leaders of civil society. A former first lady of both Mozambique and South Africa, Mrs Machel has extensive experience in both governmental and non-governmental affairs at the national, regional and international levels. Mrs Machel is currently a member of the Advisory Board on Disarmament Matters at the United Nations (UN), where she also led the team of experts that prepared a report for the UN Secretary-General on the impact of armed conflict on children. Mrs Machel is also a member of the boards of the UN Foundation, the UN University and the South Centre. Mrs Machel is Chair of the Commonwealth Foundation.

* * *

In the strategies for poverty eradication and social development, good governance has acquired a central place. Good governance implies a range of reforms – public services, judiciary, government agencies and participation of a vibrant civil society in public affairs. How do ordinary citizens view 'good governance'?

This book begins to address that question. It brings together the voices of nearly 10,000 ordinary citizens from 47 countries of the Commonwealth. These voices speak clearly and unequivocally. They point to the aspirations of ordinary people, whose dreams are rarely shared, heard or answered.

The analysis presented in this book helps to identify strategies for action in placing citizens at the centre of governance. Thus, future reforms aimed at good governance can use this reference point for citizen participation.

The findings of this book bring to our notice both similarities and differences in the developed and developing countries of the Commonwealth. What is interesting is the wide convergence in the perceptions and experiences of ordinary citizens throughout the Commonwealth. Such a coherent voice must be heard by governments. Greater participation of ordinary citizens can help towards solving problems of poverty, marginalization and discrimination.

Graça Machel
June 2001

Acknowledgements

NATIONAL PARTNERS

The following individuals and organizations carried out the research on behalf of the Commonwealth Foundation and prepared national reports.

Caribbean Region

Belize	Society for the Promotion of Education and Research
Dominica	Small Projects Assistance Team
Guyana	Red Thread Women's Development Programme
Jamaica	Association of Development Agencies
Trinidad and Tobago	Working Women for Social Progress

Africa Region

Botswana	Botswana Council of Non-Governmental Organizations
Cameroon	League for Women and Children's Education
Ghana	Integrated Social Development Centre
Kenya	The National Council of Non-Governmental Organizations
Lesotho	Sechaba Consultants
Malawi	Mr Lewis B Dzimbiri

Mauritius	Mauritius Council of Social Services
Namibia	Namibia Non-Governmental Organizations' Forum
Nigeria	Coalition for Popular Development Initiatives
Sierra Leone	Association for Rural Development
Seychelles	Liaison Unit of Non-Governmental Organizations of Seychelles
South Africa	South African National Non-Governmental Organization Coalition
Swaziland	Save the Children Fund
Tanzania	Tanzania Gender Networking
The Gambia	The Association of Non-Governmental Organizations
Uganda	Development Network of Indigenous Voluntary Associations
Zambia	Women for Change
Zimbabwe	Africa Community Publishing and Development

Pacific Region

Cook Islands	Ms Marjorie Crocombe
Fiji	Fiji Council of Social Services
Kiribati	Mr Kaburoro Tanielu/Ms Meme Tong Kiribati, Association of Non-Governmental Organizations
Nauru	Nauru Island Association of Non-Governmental Organizations
Niue	Mr Maru Talagi
Papua New Guinea	National Alliance of Non-Governmental Organizations of Papua New Guinea
Samoa	Mr Koroseta To'o
Solomon Islands	Development Services Exchange
Tonga	Mr Siosiua Po'Oi Pohiva
Tuvalu	Tuvalu National Council of Women
Vanuatu	National Community Development Trust

The Institute of Justice and Applied Legal Studies and the University Centres of the University of the South Pacific in Cook Islands, Kiribati, Niue, Tokelau, Tonga and Samoa also assisted the national partners and task force members in the Pacific region.

Asia Region

India	Society for Participatory Research in Asia
Bangladesh	PRIP (Participatory Research in Proshika)
Pakistan	South Asia Partnership – Pakistan
Sri Lanka	South Asia Partnership – Sri Lanka
Malaysia	Universiti Sains Malaysia

Developed Countries

Australia	Sydney University of Technology
Canada	Canadian Policy Research Networks
New Zealand	Association of Non-Governmental Organizations of Aotearoa Te Korowai Aroha
United Kingdom	National Council for Voluntary Organizations

Other Research

Some research was also carried out in:

Barbados	Association of Barbados Non-Governmental Organizations
Mozambique	Organizaçao de Apoio à Proteccao do Meio Ambiente e aos Desprotegidos Maputo
Tokelau	Ms Cheryl Simi
Singapore	National University of Singapore

The Eminent Persons Support Group

Mozambique	Sra Graça Machel
Canada	Mr Maurice Strong

India	Ms Ela Bhatt
New Zealand	The Hon Dame Justice Sylvia Cartwright
Barbados	Sir Clyde Walcott

FUNDERS

Commonwealth Foundation
Ford Foundation
Department for International Development (UK)
New Zealand Ministry of Foreign Affairs and Trade
New Zealand Department of Internal Affairs
Foreign and Commonwealth Office (UK)

PROGRAMME TEAM

Peta-Anne Baker, Colin Ball, Suzanne Francis-Brown, Chan Lean Heng, Rudo Chitiga, Humuyan Khan, Ezra Mbgori, Kumi Naidoo, Caren Wickliffe and Miriam Wyman

SPECIAL EDITORIAL WORK

Andrew Milner

List of Acronyms and Abbreviations

AIDS	acquired immune deficiency syndrome
CBD	Convention on Biological Diversity
CFTC	Commonwealth Fund for Technical Cooperation
CHOGM	Commonwealth Heads of Government Meeting
CIA	Central Intelligence Agency
CMAG	Ministerial Action Group of Foreign Ministers
GATT	General Agreement on Tariffs and Trade
GDP	gross domestic product
IMF	International Monetary Fund
LSE	London School of Economics
NAFTA	North American Free Trade Agreement
NGO	non-governmental organization
OAU	Organization for African Unity
ODA	Overseas Development Agency
OECD	Organization for Economic Cooperation and Development
PRIA	Society for Participatory Research in Asia
PRIP	Participatory Research in Proshika
SAARC	South Asian Association for Regional Cooperation
SANASO	Southern African Network of AIDS Organizations
SPEAR	Society for the Promotion of Education and Research (Belize)
UDHR	Universal Declaration of Human Rights
UK	United Kingdom

UN	United Nations
UNCED	United Nations Conference on Environment and Development
UNDP	United Nations Development Programme
UNHCR	United Nations High Commissioner for Refugees
UNICEF	United Nations Children's Fund
US	United States
WTO	World Trade Organization

Introduction

Democracies are losing voters. Citizens are missing from governance. Politics is everywhere failing.

Politicians of all shades of opinion are worried about the yawning gulf between political institutions and their citizens. This 'dislocation in the age of globalization' has not only found expression in recent protests against world leaders on the streets of Seattle, Washington, Davos, Gothenburg and Genoa (Norman, 2001), but has also been apparent in the withdrawal from democratic procedures, such as voting in elections, turning out for community meetings and holding public office (Putnam, 2000). The pact between governors and governed is breaking down.

What is at stake is the social contract between citizens and governments. A tacit agreement under which citizens contribute their thinking to the government's decisions and take some responsibility for those decisions once they are made, the social contract, has underpinned the development of democracy since the 18th century. It is the glue that holds our societies together (Selbourne, 1994).

With the social contract in jeopardy, we risk falling prey to the forces of barbarism. The downward spiral runs as follows: as the legitimate institutions of politics atrophy, people act out their alienation through withdrawal or violence, governments lose control and societies fail and lapse into disorder (Greider, 1992).

It is ironic that such widespread concerns should emerge only a decade after the revolutions of 1989, when the idea of democracy triumphed and became the norm to which civilized nations aspired (Fukuyama, 1992). Part of the problem has been that democracies have been too weak to manage that great engine of economic growth, capitalism – and, more especially, capitalism in its globalized form. Wealth creation has proceeded apace since 1989, bringing a burgeoning middle class in its wake so that there is now a new category of consumer targeted by financial institutions called the 'mass affluent'. At the same time, the new wealth has failed to reach billions of others, and the wealth gap between North and South remains as large as ever. The bipolar world of the great powers may have disappeared, but the bipolar world of 'haves' and 'have nots' remains. To cope with the increasing power of global capitalism, states have begun to group themselves into larger economic units across the world. However, this has removed governments still further from the people, and much of the debate about the democratic deficit focuses on supranational structures, such as the European Union (Baun, 1996).

It is increasingly clear that we cannot have everything. Ralf Dahrendorf (1997) suggests that there are three components of a good society: prosperity, civility and liberty. He indicates that you can have any two of these, but not all three. The world since 1989 has been driven by two of these forces – prosperity and liberty. The casualty has been civility. Social cohesion has declined. Witness the growing anxieties about the health of social institutions, the decline of the family, reductions in social capital, the absence of consensus on unifying moral principles and the disappearance of voluntary associations (Eberly, 2000).

The debate about civil society centres on these failings. One of the reasons for the intensity of the debate is the feeling that civil society is something that we have lost – an 'aching void', as Ernest Gellner (1994) described it. There is little doubt that the idea of civil society is an important one (Van Rooy and Robinson, 1998) and will continue to grow in importance. However, the focus of interest in the debate has been on non-governmental organizations

(NGOs). This is too restrictive and leaves out the most basic and important ingredient of civil society – its citizens.

This book tries to restore the balance by asking citizens about their views of a good society. Much of the thinking behind the study was inspired by William Greider (1992) in *Who Will Tell the People?* Our study began with a different question: who will ask the people? ⟍¡⊓⌐⌐

The sub-title of this book, *Citizens at the Heart of Governance*, gives pride of place to citizens. The contents specify the kind of society *they* want. Their views are rooted in one of the most ambitious participatory research studies ever undertaken, entitled 'Civil Society in the New Millennium' and sponsored by the Commonwealth Foundation in association with CIVICUS: The World Alliance for Citizen Participation (generally known simply as CIVICUS).

In the study, ordinary citizens from many different countries in many different settings offered their opinions about a good society. The results revealed their capacity to analyse and express their local, complex and diverse realities. Often, their perspectives were at odds with the top-down view of reality imposed upon them, and suggested that many mistakes have flowed from this view. In many cases, local people were able to suggest practical and workable solutions to the problems they face, identifying roles for government, other institutions and themselves.

WHY LISTEN TO CITIZENS?

The Commonwealth exists for its citizens. Through the 'Civil Society in the New Millennium' study, the Commonwealth Foundation investigated their hopes and dreams so that it might plan to begin to meet them. Among all sectors of society across the world, there is increasing recognition that successful societies depend upon involving people as partners. In some parts of the world, people have begun to opt out of social, economic and political life, creating a crisis of governability and threatening the legitimacy of the state. In other parts of the world, the fabric of society is stretched so much that persistent conflict threatens to engulf entire countries and regions. In all areas of the world, governments face a resource crisis, so that they cannot do all that they would like to do, and in many cases are having to cut back. In many countries, particularly in the global South, the resource crisis is caused by debt, inability to compete in the global market place or structural adjustment programmes. In other countries, notably in the global North, the resource crisis is due to the unwillingness of citizens to pay more tax to fund government programmes. In many parts of the world, citizens have tended to retreat away from the public domain, leaving their governments to govern, but with little respect for what those governments do.

This situation carries many dangers. The remedy, as this book shows, is greater citizen involvement in the public domain.

SPECIAL FEATURES OF THIS BOOK

This book is based on a two-year research study called 'Civil Society in the New Millennium', sponsored by the Commonwealth Foundation. Using a variety of participatory techniques at local, regional and international levels, and involving an international, multicultural team of researchers, the research sought the views of 10,000 citizens in 47 countries of the Commonwealth and gleaned from them a description of their idea of a good society and how to achieve it. A full account of the research methods is given in Chapter 2.

A Commonwealth Foundation Task Force led the work, while a national team conducted the research in each of the countries. Citizens in these countries were asked three questions:

1   What is your view of a 'good' society? To what extent does such a society exist today?

2   What roles are best played by citizens and what roles are best played by the state and other sectors in such a 'good' society?

3   What would enable citizens to play their role in the development of society more effectively in future?

The study was undertaken at the turn of the millennium. The Commonwealth Foundation along with many other people and organizations, used this transitional point to reflect on changes taking place across the globe to plan future work programmes.

Outputs published so far include 47 country reports, 5 regional syntheses (from Africa, Asia, the Caribbean, the Pacific and the developed countries) and a global synthesis called *Citizens and Governance: Civil Society in the New Millennium*. This book draws on all of these materials to create a detailed overview. The study complements recent studies of poor citizens undertaken by the World Bank (Narayan, 2000; Narayan et al, 2000) and reaches similar conclusions; but it also differs from these studies by including material from citizens with higher status and some with real influence in their societies.

The results of the research shake up the established ways of looking at social, economic and political issues, ushering in a new way of bridging the gap between theory and practice. Preliminary results from the research were discussed by the Third Commonwealth Non-Governmental Organization (NGO) Forum held in Durban, South Africa, in November 1999. The research informed the drafting of a communiqué to the Commonwealth Heads of Government Meeting that took place shortly afterwards. When they met, the Commonwealth Heads of Government asked for the recommendations of the research to be implemented.

The results of the research have been used to form the baseline for a developmental programme across the Commonwealth, which began in 2000 and for which a conference is planned for 2002. Results will be reported to a high-level conference in which leaders from government, business and civil society will develop a new relationship between citizens and governance.

ORGANIZATION OF THIS BOOK

Chapter 1, 'The Good Society in the Global Context', sets out an overview of the world, describing the rise of civil society and the attendant social, economic and political trends.

Chapter 2, 'Civil Society and Participatory Research', describes the logic and techniques of participatory research and how these relate to civil society.

Chapter 3, 'The Good Society', reports on what citizens want and develops a model based on what they say.

Chapter 4, 'Friends and Enemies of the Good Society', sets out factors that help or hinder the attainment of the 'good' society.

Chapter 5, 'Good Governance', focuses on what governments, citizens and others can do to create a 'good' society.

Chapter 6, 'What Is To Be Done?', suggests next steps and sets out what the Commonwealth Foundation will do in the future.

1

The Good Society in a Global Context

INTRODUCTION

This chapter sets the idea of a good society against the background of current global political, economic and cultural trends. We will see that, despite the upheavals of the 20th century, its last decade produced a common consensus about how to develop societies, based on the interaction of state, market and civil society. However, we show how the civil society component of this model has, so far, left out its most vital ingredient – namely, the participation of citizens. The current study fills the gap.

THE GOOD SOCIETY

The idea of a good society has occupied some of the finest minds in history, certainly since the time of Ancient Egypt and probably before (Nowell-Smith, 1954).[1] Controversies have raged about whether a good society could ever exist. Broadly speaking, the debate divides between utopians and realists.

Edmund Burke was among the first to attack utopian attempts to draw up a blueprint of what a good society would be like and to make it into a reality. Such attempts were at odds with 'reason, and order, and peace, and virtue, and fruitful penitence', and would lead to 'madness, discord, vice, confusion and unavailing sorrow' (Burke, 1790). Anti-utopian sentiments came to the fore after the Russian Revolution of 1917, particularly through the writings of Walter Lippman, Friedrich Hayek, Sir Karl Popper and Seymour Martin Lipsett, all of whom saw utopianism as a dangerous illusion (Arblaster and Lukes, 1971). In the period after World War II, Anthony Crosland's influential *The Future of Socialism* attacked 'the vulgar fallacy that some ideal society can be said to exist, of which blueprints can be drawn, and which will be ushered in as soon as certain specific reforms have been delivered' (Crosland, 1955).

One of the reasons why such realism abhors attempts to realize a utopian vision is that it involves a commitment to a planned society. This is regarded either as impossible, because of the sheer complexity of social phenomena, or undesirable because it restricts the freedom of individuals.

Ironically, most of the utopians, whether communist (Karl Marx or Vladimir Lenin), socialist (Robert Owen or William Morris) or anarchist (Pierre Joseph Proudhon or Peter Kropotkin) had visions of society based on the voluntary principle, in which equal wealth, status and power depended upon what people wanted rather than imposition by rules, law or authority. As Lenin put it, 'So long as the state exists there is no freedom. When there is freedom, there will be no state' (Lenin, 1917).

The difference between utopians and realists is essentially a moral one. The realists look on what Michael Oakeshott called 'the current condition of human circumstances' with relative satisfaction, or at least with passive resignation (Oakeshott, 1956). They believe that either current circumstances merit no significant improvement or to attempt such improvement would amount to interfering folly. Utopians, on the other hand, have their eyes firmly fixed on the grim reality of social and economic oppression and wish to change it. Oscar Wilde wrote (1891):

> *A map of the world that does not include Utopia is not worth even glancing at, for it leaves out the one country at*

which Humanity is always landing. And when Humanity lands there, it looks out, and, always seeing a better country, sets sail. Progress is the realization of Utopias.

Ultimately the argument is a normative one that focuses, firstly, on whether or not we can make progress and, secondly, on whether we wish to do so. The first question is, 'Do we believe in progress?' The second is, 'Do we want to create progress?'

The argument so far takes an entirely Western and, most particularly, a European view of the debate. From the South, particularly from Africa, Asia and the Pacific, the issues are entirely different. Here, the debate on what constitutes a good society tends to focus on the conflict between tradition and modernity. Indeed, the essence of a good society is often seen in conserving tradition and in warding off modernity. Far from being the essence of a good society, progress is here seen as an enemy.

In considering traditional culture, it is important to beware of falling into the trap of stereotypes (Pandey, 1993), or believing that traditional cultures have remained static for many centuries until the present one (Dietrich, 1989), or believing that traditional culture is homogeneous (Kapen, 1994).

Indeed, it is important to speak of cultures in the plural, since, as Kapen (1994) points out, traditional culture:

... is anything but a homogeneous whole, containing, as it does, varied and conflicting tendencies – the Vedic and the Tantric, the patriarchal and the matriarchal, the Saivite and the Vaishnavite, the Orthodox and the heterodox, the indigenous and the exogenous.

Moreover, these remarks are restricted solely to Asian cultures. Variations would be even greater if traditional cultures from other parts of the world were included. The empirical data, reported later, consider a variety of traditional cultures from many parts of the world.

Regardless of location, there appear to be six factors that are commonly present in traditional cultures that distinguish their ways of life from those in the North and West. These are as follows:

1   *Primacy of community versus primacy of the individual.* In traditional cultures, individuals are subservient to the needs of the family, clan, caste or tribe, rather than being free to pursue their own destiny, which tends to be the norm in modern societies.

2   *Hierarchy of birth versus hierarchy of merit.* In traditional cultures, aspirations are determined largely by the family, clan, caste or tribe, rather than through competition or meritorious performance, which tends to be the norm in modern societies.

3   *Work as worship versus work as profit.* In traditional cultures, work is conducted because it is useful and meaningful in its own right, rather than because of its commercial value, which tends to be the motivation in modern societies.

4   *Simplicity versus complexity.* In traditional cultures, needs are met in a holistic and simple way, rather than through the modern consumer market and its attendant complexity.

5   *Myth versus logic.* In traditional cultures, part of the story of human existence is spiritual, transcending everyday experience, so that one walks with God, gods or goddesses, whereas modern societies tend to use analytical procedures based on a logical positivist frame of reference deriving from the tradition of Ayer (1937).

6   *Cyclical versus linear.* In traditional cultures, life follows the rhythm of natural cycles of day and night, growth and decay, life and death, rather than the linear models of progress that tend to be used in modern societies.

Taken together, these characteristics are thought by many to indicate a good society. At the same time, people who advocate this view are not so naïve as to consider that all elements of a traditional society are good. Take, for example, Ponna Wignaraja and Akmal Hussein (1989), who have written a lucid account of some of the traditional communities of South Asia. They suggest that the best features of traditional societies involve a deep-rooted posture of tolerance, a highly evolved humanism and an ethos in which linguistic, religious or ethnic groups can tolerate and appreciate the creative elements of others. These humanist traits find expression in a rich folk tradition and artistic ritual, through which fundamental wellsprings of love and creativity spill over, finding expression in unity through diversity. Wignaraja and Hussein cite Barba Farid, a 13th-century poet, who expresses this idea:

In every form I see my beloved
My heart is lost in my beloved.

At the same time, Wignaraja and Hussein point out that traditional communities contain the potential to displace this humanist perspective and fall prey to fear, intolerance and aggression. The trigger is almost always a threat – real or imagined – posed by another community. When people in any given community feel that their very survival is threatened, humanitarian impulses can flip over into hostile ones. The result is the communal conflict and civil strife that has characterized the history of South Asia. The underlying significance of such communal conflict is that people are willing to die for their vision of a good society when it is threatened by outside forces.

Communal conflict is commonly made worse by progress based on the Western model. The centralization of political power, the development of cultural homogeneity and the forging of large economic units for the purposes of capital accumulation, market coherence and productive capacity bring outside political and economic interests into play. New political administrations, particularly of the colonial variety, have usually ridden roughshod over local tribal or community divisions. In many parts of Africa, for example, nation states were fashioned out of arbitrary divisions of territory by colonial powers. It was common to use lines of latitude and longitude, rather than the perceptions of local people. Moreover, these imposed arrangements involved forcible unification, as well as forcible division. Most existing African polities were smaller than the European colonies that replaced them; as a result, different political units were often treated as one by their colonial rulers without regard for their differences. To develop the economies of the new states, colonial powers usually effected a transition from the subsistence to the market economy, a process that tended to make local communities poorer because the market system filtered wealth upwards and out of the local economy into the hands of the local and international elite, who pocketed surplus value from the efforts of primary producers in villages. Political elites often managed the resulting economic distress among local communities through a policy of divide and rule, setting one local community against another and unleashing the psychic forces that produce communal violence (Gurr, 1993).

Colonialism and its sense of progress brought a new and unsympathetic worldview to traditional communities. For many people in the South, the idea of a good society is still bound up with traditional values. For them, notions of modernity and progress connote the opposite of a good society because progress destroys what they hold dear. However, in the past, the views of the South have had little influence on theories concerning how the world has developed; over the past two decades, such theories have been dominated by what John Williamson of the Institute for International Economics called the 'Washington consensus' (Edwards, 1999).

THE CURRENT CONSENSUS

There is a broad consensus among the world's elites, including major international donors, government leaders and think tanks, about how to develop societies across the world.[2] The model has three components.

First, *democracy* is seen as the best form of government. With ever more countries adopting democracy (Fukuyama, 1992; Mbogori and Chigudu, 1999; Myers, 1999), the state is expected to devolve some of its powers and resources to local bodies and to shed some of its functions in the direct management of economic and social activities (World Bank, 1996). In short, governments are expected to move to a type of governance, defined in this book as 'collective decision-making in which government acts as one stakeholder among many' (Hague et al, 1998; World Bank, 1997).

Second, *private enterprise* in the free market is identified as the primary engine of economic development. This involves the acceptance of capitalism and measures to promote it, such as enhancing the role of foreign investment in developing countries and the deregulation of trade (World Bank, 1996).

Third, *civil society* is given a paramount role. The last years of the 20th century have seen the rebirth of the idea of civil society (Cohen and Arato, 1992). In turn, this has led to an explosion of interest in NGOs, women's organizations, cooperatives, self-help groups and other types of civil society organization, both secular and religious (Salamon et al, 1999; CIVICUS, 1999; McCarthy et al, 1991; D'Olivera and Tandon, 1995). These actors are expected to play a greater role in the development process in many parts of the world. Among countries taking this line are the Philippines (Serrano, 1994; Diokno, 1997), Japan (Tadashi, 1999), Bangladesh (Mammoon and Ray, 1998), India (Indian Social Institute, 1997; Gulhati and Gulhati, 1999; Nagaraja and Bhat, 2000), Sri Lanka (Abeysekera and Weerakoon, 1996) and New Zealand (Davenport and Low, 1999). Civil society is also seen as an important regional development strategy, and has been proposed across the Asia Pacific region (Yamamoto, 1995), in Africa (CIVICUS, 1999; Olin, 1995; Mugunga, 1999; Nyang'oro, 1999) and Central and Eastern Europe (Les, 1994; Seegal and Yancey, 1992). Official agencies have also

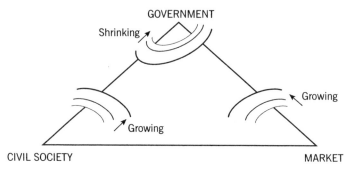

Figure 1.1 *Current consensus towards a good society*

encouraged NGOs to become involved in development (World Bank, 1990, 1991; Sherma, 1991; UNDP, 1997; UNDP, 1999).

This current consensus – three players creating a new model of a good society – is represented graphically in Figure 1.1.

CRACKS IN THE CONSENSUS

Cracks have appeared in the consensus since it reached its apotheosis during 1990–1997. The Asian crisis of 1997 gave a severe jolt to confidence in free markets, and led to discussions at the World Economic Forum in January 1998 about how to regulate the free flow of capital. Such anxieties found their way into World Bank development reports, leading to an about-turn on the matter of regulation (World Bank, 1999). Subsequent reports, particularly *Attacking Poverty*, have given a higher profile to social matters and have been based on consultations with poor people, NGOs and other groupings (World Bank, 2000). Indeed, there is now a 'new Washington consensus' (Edwards, 1999). Fiscal discipline remains, though it is balanced by more attention to social expenditure and education, institution building, global regulation and debt relief. Everyone now speaks the language of participation, gender equity, sustainability and poverty reduction, though whether practice has changed is a different question.

Concerns about poverty, instability and inequity have enhanced the importance of civil society as the third force in the model. Nevertheless, almost all of the references in official documents point to the contribution of NGOs, despite the fact that they form only a part of civil society and, according to a recent World Bank study, tend to have only limited impact on the lives of many people (Narayan, 2000). In part, a concentration on NGOs reflects the fact that the Washington consensus is a view from the top, and that NGOs are the most visible part of civil society from that standpoint.

There is, moreover, increasing recognition that models of development are subject to fashion and faith. Development theory has little to say about how to reconcile economic, social and political forces to produce desirable outcomes. There is little sense of good practice, sound advice or hard evaluative evidence to guide the way. Indeed, the Washington consensus has been described as a 'myth driven by a powerful elite' (Edwards, 1999).[3]

This openness may lead in the direction of a people-centred consensus, and the merit of the current debate about civil society is that it opens that door. It is striking that the last occasion when the idea of civil society came to prominence was 200 years ago, as society was shifting from an agricultural to an industrial economy, and from a feudal to a capitalist society. The thrust of the 18th-century Enlightenment was to replace a society based on feudal forms of economic obligation, military power and religious intolerance with a society based on scientific understanding, commercialism and civil society. During the Enlightenment, civil society was contrasted with religious or military society (Schechter, 1999).

The notion of civil society has reappeared just as we are going through another transition. This time the shifts are, variously, from authoritarian regimes to liberal democracies, and from industrial society to the information age. Civil society is here contrasted with the state and the market economy. It is clear from experience that civil society and the market economy do not always dovetail as neatly as the model in Figure 1.1 might wish to suggest.

First, we have to understand the terms of the current debate as it relates to the underlying transitions taking place across the globe, particularly in the economy and the state. These topics form the remainder of the chapter.

GLOBAL ECONOMIC TRENDS

Population

The world's population has doubled during the past 40 years, reaching six billion in July 1999 (US Census Estimate, 1999). Although growth has now slowed, it is still expanding at 78 million per annum, with predictions of 8.9 billion people in the year 2050 and 11 billion in the year 2200. This has led to pessimistic accounts of 'the coming anarchy' due to overpopulation and environmental degradation (Kaplan, 1994). However, the death rates caused by the HIV/AIDS pandemic in some countries of the South, such as Zimbabwe, Botswana, South Africa, Zambia and Uganda, suggest that such fears may be misplaced and that different causes for concern may become paramount.

Economic growth

Population growth has, by and large, been supported by economic growth. Average per-capita incomes have tripled in the past 50 years as global gross domestic product (GDP) – the world's total production of goods and services – has increased from US$3 trillion to US$30 trillion (United Nations, 1999). This growth has created a burgeoning middle class who now make up nearly one third of the world's population (Central Intelligence Agency, 2000).

Inequality

Growth, however, has been uneven. In 1997, the richest 20 per cent of nations produced 86 per cent of global GDP, while the poorest

20 per cent produced 1 per cent, creating huge and increasing disparities in income and wealth (United Nations, 1998).

Poverty

The result is widespread poverty. Some 1.3 billion people (more than 20 per cent of the world's population) live on less than US$1 per day. About 840 million (14 per cent) are malnourished.

Regional contrasts

There are stark regional contrasts. Eight of the world's ten poorest nations are in Africa, alongside Bangladesh and Nepal in South Asia.

Let us contrast East Asia with Sub-Saharan Africa. In the years between 1960 and 1992, East Asia increased its share of global GDP from 4 per cent to 25 per cent. Led by Japan, the four East Asian 'tigers' (Hong Kong, Singapore, South Korea and Taiwan) offered foreign investors an appealing combination of cheap labour and stable politics. In contrast, the countries of Sub-Saharan Africa have remained 'out of the game' (Palan and Abbott, 1996). There has been no growth, and even states with the cheapest labour and stable politics have failed to attract foreign investment.

Measures undertaken to improve the situation have often made matters worse. Economic structural adjustment has led to de-industrialization, unemployment, a fall in real wages for workers, rising food prices, increasing debt burdens, heavy budget deficits and a decline in welfare services in many countries of Africa (Tandon, 1997). The international aid system has failed to make inroads into the problem for a variety of reasons (Edwards, 1999; Leys, 1996). Aid efficiency is constantly being eroded by a lack of targeting, poor coordination among donor and state agencies and persistent armed conflict. Contributory factors include the continuing legacy of colonialism, bad government and corruption.

In-country contrasts

There are marked disparities, too, within countries. In India, for example, the rate of poverty in the state of Bihar is more than twice that of Kerala. Contrasts are even more marked in developed countries, where the proportion of people who live in poverty ranges from one in eight to one in three.

Technology

Since Adam Smith wrote the first modern treatise on economics in 1776, a tenet of economic growth has been to replace people with machines in the agricultural or industrial process. During the past two decades, however, the pace of change has amounted to a technological revolution, resulting in near instantaneous global communications and rapidly falling transaction costs.

Media

One of the effects of this technological explosion is the instant availability of news coverage. This has changed the way in which the world works and the speed at which it reacts. One expression of this is the phenomenon known as the CNN curve. When the 24-hour Cable News Network reports news of a foreign crisis, it evokes an emotional outcry from the public and forces politicians to respond. Such coverage is commonly highly selective, focusing on the interests of the global North (Bell, 1995).

While there has been a proliferation of media outlets, the number of owners of media companies has shrunk (Mowlana, 1995). From 50 major corporations in the early 1980s, there are now only 20. This has led to suggestions that a small number of individuals have undue influence on how the world thinks (Bagkikian, 1992).

The 'new economy'

Another by-product of technological advance is the creation of a 'new economy' (*The Economist*, 1999). American companies massively increased their annual investment in computers during the 1990s, with the result that the high-tech sector of the economy has accounted for 35 per cent of US growth. Computer software companies in the United States now employ 800,000 people, and it is predicted that by 2006 half of US workers will be employed in the information technology industry (US Government Commerce Department, 1999). Other countries in the world have followed suit. A notable example is the Republic of Ireland, where investment in computer-related products has led to growth rates of 7 per cent over the past decade, earning Ireland the nickname of 'the Celtic Tiger'.

The new economy fuelled the stock market, using 'virtual money' whose sole function is to make more money (Drucker, 1997); in the process, it helped to create the longest running bull market that the United States has ever known. There were fears that large investment in companies who had yet to make a profit would produce 'a bubble' (Arthur, 1999), and such fears were realized during 2000 when the bubble burst, leading to serious falls in the stock market.

Labour market

The new economy has wrought changes in the labour market. Many of the older trades have disappeared, and solidarity between workers – expressed through trade unions – has been replaced by competition. The global labour market has still to assimilate the full impact of the recent influx of three giant populations – China, the former Soviet Union and India.

There is a worldwide oversupply of labour, and unskilled labour is virtually worthless, with women often being worst hit. One third of the world's 2.8 billion workers are unemployed or underemployed. Many have low wages with little prospect for advancement (Marshall, 1995). The situation is worse in the southern parts of the globe, though ameliorated to some degree by the tendency for multinational companies to target investment in countries of the South.

GLOBALIZATION

Globalization has been called 'globaloney' on the grounds that it is a woolly term used to lump together many different and superficially converging trends (Strange, 1995). It is a word used by elites who tend to forget that half of the world has yet to make its first telephone call (*Christian Science Monitor*, 1995). However, although we are still a long way from Marshall McLuhan's 'global village' (McLuhan, 1962), it is clear that geography has shifted under our feet within a generation, and there has been a profound 'intensification of economic, political, social and cultural relations across borders' (Holm and Sorensen, 1995).

Globalization has been uneven, with the vast bulk of trade occurring between Organization for Economic Cooperation and Development (OECD) countries or the richer countries of South-East Asia (*The Economist*, 1998). Many of the countries of South Asia, Africa and the Pacific regions are still largely traditional agrarian economies (United Nations, 1999), and some have yet to make the transition from subsistence to cash economies. In these countries, vast numbers of people have no direct contact with the sophisticated credit-based economies that middle-class people in the West take for granted.

It appears that the wealth-creation machine is out of control. Of the world's 100 largest economies, 51 are private companies (Vida, 1997). The globalization of mass communications, production and marketing has tended to speed up the spread of Western secular and consumerist values. This has led to a 'cultural revolution involving the triumph of the individual over society or, rather, the breaking of the threads which in the past had woven human beings into social textures' (Hobsbawm, 1994). Korten (1995) has noted the downside of this process. He gives the example of Pakistan, where elites live in enclaves detached from local roots. The country's three modern cities – Karachi, Lahore and Islamabad – contain enclaves of five-star hotels, modern shopping malls and posh residential areas. Yet just outside of these areas there is a poor and feudalistic countryside governed by local lords who support private armies with profits from a thriving drug-and-arms trade and who are inclined to kill any central government official who dares to enter.

There are a few countervailing influences to the march of capitalism. The main one is Islam. We saw earlier that traditional societies and indigenous peoples tend to oppose such progress. And demonstrations at Seattle in 1999 in response to the meeting of the World Trade Organization (WTO) that year, followed by similar protests in other cities, suggest that there is some organized opposition. But how did capitalism take such a hold?

THE RISE OF FREEDOM

To answer this question, we need to go back to the Bretton Woods meeting of 1944, which set the terms of the economic peace and initiated the World Bank and the International Monetary Fund (IMF). The premise of these arrangements was that nation states should be free to plan their domestic economies. To prevent external disturbance, capital from one country would not cross the border into another without the agreement of the governments concerned. The two key words were 'planning' and 'domestic'. A famous post-war dictum was, 'We are all planners now' (Dublin, 1949). Previously, the *laissez faire* doctrine of 19th-century philosopher John Stuart Mill held sway over the minds of economists. The essence of his view was (Mill, 1848):

Laissez faire *should be the general practice: every departure from it, unless required by some great good, is a certain evil.*

The Wall Street Crash of 1929, followed by the Great Depression of the 1930s, had caused so much pain and suffering that a seismic shift took place in the minds of politicians. Capitalist economies needed planning (Keynes, 1936).

For 30 years after the war, Keynes and Marx walked in step. Then, in the mid-1970s, the West broke with Keynes and a decade later the East broke with Marx. Mill had mounted a posthumous rearguard action through a right-wing disciple, Friedrich von Hayek, who suggested that the market is the ultimate arbiter of virtue. Capitalist society is the highest society because it has evolved and survived, while other societies lacking the traditions, habits and structures of the capitalist order have failed in the competition between human groups (Hayek, 1988).

The ideas of Hayek were quoted approvingly both by Ronald Reagan when he was US president and by Margaret Thatcher when she was UK prime minister. Through these means, the ideas of Hayek have had a huge effect on the economic organization of the world.

Why did this happen? The answer has as much to do with pragmatic action as with political philosophy. In 1971, the United States had heavy debts, partly because of the expense of the Vietnam War. This meant that the United States could no longer meet its commitment to translate its dollar obligations into gold. From there, it was a short step to abandoning the fixed exchange rate mechanisms under Bretton Woods, and this happened in 1973. This opened the door to international currency speculation and led to huge fluctuations in currency prices and commodity values. Oil price inflation, as a result of the Arab–Israeli war, meant that some nations built up huge dollar reserves while others built up debts. The world's economy was out of balance (Leys, 1996).

Nation-state economics could not hold up against this pressure. During 1979–1980 the OECD, led by the UK and the United States, abandoned Keynes. They opted instead for deregulation and privatization. For a time, France stood against this but had to capitulate in 1983. This was a symbolic moment. The era of Bretton Woods was over and, as one commentator put it, 'the world was turned upside down' (Helleiner, 1994).

By the end of the 1980s, financiers were dealing not only in conventional transactions needed for trade and investment, but also in a wide range of currency and commodity futures and derivatives. It was ironic that financial instruments, such as futures, which were originally designed to create stability in the global market, later created instability because of the tendency for speculators to gamble on whether they would rise or fall.

In 1993, the Uruguay Round of the General Agreement on Tariffs and Trade (GATT) extended global free trade to the formerly sacrosanct agricultural sector. At the same time, the Maastricht Treaty of the European Union and the North American Free Trade Agreement (NAFTA) further reduced the regulatory powers of nation states in the global economy.

While the capitalist world was liberalizing itself, the communist bloc began its first faltering steps along the same route. *Perestroika* (economic restructuring) in the Soviet Union began as a means of altering the balance between three forms of ownership in the economy: state enterprises, state cooperatives and household economies (the family plot of land). At first, the idea was to strengthen state cooperatives and household economies. Gradually, *Perestroika* widened into a programme to deregulate the economy and to enable individuals to set up small businesses (Andrusz, 1999). This programme, combined with its close political relative *Glasnost* (openness), set in train a series of events that was to bring an end to communism as a viable form of social and economic organization.

During the 1980s, the world was converging in the direction of greater freedom, both economically and politically. In 1989, the year that the Berlin Wall came down, Francis Fukuyama wrote an influential article called the 'End of History?', followed by a very influential book, *The End of History and the Last Man*. He suggested that the idea of liberal democracy had triumphed, replacing competitors, including hereditary monarchy, fascism and, most significantly, communism (Fukuyama, 1989; 1992). Hegel, not Marx, had got the upper hand.

At the Malta Summit in December 1989, Presidents Bush and Gorbachev announced the end of the Cold War. There followed a brief period when it seemed as if a new and positive world was opening up. The collapse of the Berlin Wall, the ending of Apartheid in South Africa, the liberalization of regimes in South America and the spread of 'just and honest' government following the 1991 Harare Declaration by Commonwealth Heads of Government created a new agenda. Democracy was in prospect in many parts of the world. The marketplace based on consumer choice would create prosperity. There would be no war because the democratic market economies would have few ideological differences to fight about. Such hopes did not last for long.

THE DOWNSIDES OF FREEDOM

War

What destroyed the optimism was, in a word, Yugoslavia. Once the communist tyranny was shaken off, another was laid bare, this time harder and deeper: racism. Freed from central state controls, ethnic rivalries surfaced that were fed by unscrupulous politicians hungry for power. The Balkans acted out their stereotype and split in all manner of directions. Hard on the heels of Yugoslavia, there followed a bloodstained sequence of disasters in other countries ending in 'a' – Somalia, Chechnya, Rwanda, Albania, Cambodia, Indonesia, Angola, Algeria, Eritrea and Ethiopia.

Since 1989 there have been 96 major violent conflicts, and 91 of them have been civil wars, often in the form of communal violence between ethnic groups (Serrano, 1998). Such conflicts tend to be low level, persistent and resistant to formal means of intervention (Van Creveld, 1991). Cultural conflicts are claimed to be at the root of much of the difficulty (Huntingdon, 1996). The decline of the nation state and the growth of local or regional identities have been potent forces, too, with Czechoslovakia, Ethiopia, the Soviet Union and Yugoslavia breaking up under the strain. The survival of many other states remains in question, including Italy, Turkey, Indonesia, Congo, Sri Lanka and India. Some ethnic groups, for example the Kurds, live in regions that cross state lines, so that the entire region is unstable.

War was only one downside of the new globalized order. There were others.

Refugees

Although the phenomenon of refugees is old – the term was first used to describe the flight of Protestant Huguenots from France in 1685 (*The Economist*, 1999) – numbers have increased dramatically in the past decade. In 1998, the United Nations High Commissioner for Refugees (UNHCR) estimated that there were 12 million refugees around the world, as well as one million asylum seekers, 3.5 million recently returned refugees and millions more displaced within their own countries.

With the passing of the Cold War, the symbolic value of refugees from communist countries has declined. Often refugees are forced into makeshift camps in neighbouring countries who do not want them. For this reason, refugees are increasingly used as tools of war, as happened in the expulsions from Kosovo in 2000, which threatened the stability of the entire Balkan region.

The refugee crisis in Africa is a major obstacle to human development. As the recent events in the Great Lakes region have demonstrated, the refugee crisis is caused by armed conflict and further escalates such conflict, disrupting economic activities and with disastrous consequences for women and children.

Drugs

From shoot-outs in the ghettoes of Baltimore to bombs exploding on the streets of Bogota, most cities in the world now have a drug problem. Again, while the use of illegal drugs is not new – opium was a sovereign cure for ailments as diverse as diarrhoea and depression in Victorian England (Booth, 1998) – their growth is extraordinary.

Americans spend US$60 billion on illegal drugs each year. Some 400,000 people are in jail for drug offences, and Chicago's county court is open 24 hours a day to process the number of new cases. Such problems have led to a war on drugs, spearheaded by the United States. Measures include criminal investigations, financial incentives to farmers to plant passion fruit rather than coca, frequent complaints to heroin-producing nations, such as Pakistan, and military support to the government of Colombia in its civil war against the drug barons.

Despite this, the international gangs of 'black hats' who run the business remain firmly in control. They exploit their own people while exporting death and mayhem to the young and dispossessed of the world's cities. Organized crime is one of the growth areas of the world's economy, dominating some emerging economies, as in parts of the former Soviet bloc, and threatening war zones, such as Kosovo (Rozen, 1998).

HIV/AIDS

AIDS is probably the most 'international' disease there has ever been (Annan, 1999). Fourteen million people have died so far. At present, 33 million people have AIDS or are HIV positive, with 16,000 new cases of HIV infection each day. Three-quarters of people infected come from Africa. In some countries, such as Kenya, Tanzania, Zimbabwe and Uganda, the disease has reached pandemic proportions and has had deleterious effects on their economies since so many people of working age are incapacitated.

Asia is now set to see a huge AIDS explosion, with numbers of HIV cases expected to double in the next ten years. India already has more people infected than any other country in the world.

The use of a cocktail of strong drugs to manage HIV has led to falls in death rates in the West. However, the drugs are expensive and those affected in developing countries cannot afford them. Clearly, prevention here is better than any attempted cure; but ignorance, poverty, drug use, hopelessness, insecurity, subordination of women and prostitution are formidable obstacles to this.

Ecology

Many countries now suffer from environmental degradation, to the extent that commentators talk of a global environmental catastrophe (Watkins, 1995). Nigeria, for example, suffers from deforestation, overgrazing, soil erosion, waste accumulation, air and water pollution, as well as fuelwood scarcity. Hatiya Island, in the mouth of the Bay of Bengal and home to 300,000 people, faces extinction. Already coping with cyclones and tidal surges, the island is likely to disappear or become uninhabitable if global warming continues at its present rate.

The 1992 Earth Summit in Rio de Janeiro produced Agenda 21, a 500-page global action plan for achieving sustainable development. Unfortunately, little of substance has been achieved, though some improvements at the margin have been recorded. Since the United Nations Conference on Environment and Development (UNCED), the majority of the world's states are signatories to the Convention on Biodiversity (CBD). In the main, however, industrial nations have been, to a great extent, unwilling to sacrifice their lifestyle, and Agenda 21 was non-binding, with little in the way of finance for implementation.

MARKETS AND STATE ARE NOT ENOUGH

What these five issues – war, refugees, drugs, AIDS and ecology – have in common is that the problem in each case, and any solutions, lie partly outside the bailiwick of the nation state and require a great deal of international attention. Books, deals, disease, email, food, films, genes, ideas, images, information, migrants, money, music, pollution, radiation, software, students, technology, tourists, values, weapons – all cross national borders every day. Problems that once could be solved within states now require international attention. The Bretton Woods intergovernmental organizations, comprised of the World Bank, the WTO and the IMF have not been able to cope with these pressures.

The twin pillars of the new era in world politics – free market economics and liberal democracy – seem to have failed to bring the desired solutions. The vaunted giants have, in many respects, feet of clay.

Since we are all producers and consumers who act in accord with supply and demand, the idea of progress and perfectibility are unknown in free market economics. The tonic note is competition, not justice. The corrective of Adam Smith's 'invisible hand' has too often proved to be empty (Ignatieff, 1999). The opening of McDonald's' first restaurant in Wenceslas Square in Prague, where the crowds thronged to bring down the government in 1989, caused many people to ask whether 1989 had been a pyrrhic victory. Had the new world just been fashioned for the transglobal corporation?

The answer appears to be yes. However, this seems to imply both inequitable distribution of resources and persistent turbulence. Despite the gains in East Asia, the financial crash of 1997 not only created a swathe of new poor overnight, it also did untold damage to the assets built up over the previous quarter century. In the years since the Asian crisis, major difficulties have occurred in Russia and Brazil, and even anniversaries of the crashes are sufficient to create jitters in the market (Thornton, 1999).

The world's top capitalists are beginning to learn that this is a bad way in which to run a world (Ascherson, 1997). At the Davos Economic Forum, attended by the world's business leaders in 1998, the main topic for discussion was corporate responsibility (Giddens, 1999). In the political arena, too, some of the more enlightened world leaders are beginning to see an opportunity for reviewing our understanding of democracy. Pippa Norris, at Harvard University's Kennedy School of Government, hails the advent of a new breed of 'critical citizens' who see that existing channels of participation fall short of democratic ideals and want to reform them (Norris, 1999). There is a growing sense among political leaders that they need their citizens and they need to engage with them in more creative ways. Doubts about the effectiveness of market economics and liberal democracy offer an opportunity for civil society that is the central topic of our inquiry.

CHAPTER 2

Civil Society and Participatory Research

INTRODUCTION

In this chapter we turn to civil society. As we saw in Chapter 1, states and markets are insufficient on their own to develop societies successfully. Many people have suggested that a third force or sector, called civil society, is also needed.

We suggest that the top-down, quasi-scientific methods of conventional academic inquiry have so far failed to give an adequate account of civil society. As a result, the debate about civil society has reached an impasse.

The current study used participatory research methodology, consulting more than 10,000 citizens about their view of a good society. The main unit of analysis in such a methodology is what citizens say, so that definitions have the authenticity and legitimacy of wide usage among the central actors of civil society. The results throw new light on the idea of civil society and enable us to reframe that idea in the light of what citizens say about it.

HOW SHOULD WE STUDY CIVIL SOCIETY?

Chapter 1 examined how the inclusion of civil society as a third force alongside the state and the market modified the Washington consensus about how to develop the world. Ideas of civil society have now been assimilated, to some extent, by major development institutions, such as the World Bank and the European Union, as well as by some of the leading international charitable foundations. However, there have been criticisms of the approaches taken by such development agencies. Alan Fowler has pointed out that, during the 1990s, the aid system developed a 'mirror view' of civil society, creating the institutions and organizations who produced democracy in the West with little regard for the special conditions that apply to transitional states or less developed countries in the East and South (Fowler, 1997). Moreover, the establishment view of civil society is a narrow one, more or less restricted to the role of NGOs, so that the concerns of ordinary people and their views of a good society are omitted. This approach leaves out the most crucial element of civil society – citizens.

The study was designed to correct this by offering a subaltern view of the world that would go to the heart of such issues as participation, gender equity, sustainability and poverty reduction. The objective was to include the opinions of citizens, who are normally invisible, and to enlist their help in formulating a new people-centred consensus.

Civil society and participatory research (the chosen study method) are highly congruent ideas (Pateman, 1970). Common to almost all definitions of civil society is the idea of a 'sphere of interaction' between different actors in the public domain (Cohen and Arato, 1992), and participatory research involves similar interaction in the public domain.

Participatory research differs from conventional research because its techniques are used not only to understand the nature of a good society, but also to bring it into effect. In the process of studying civil society, the object is to change civil society.

Participatory research works as an agent of positive change because it possesses three interlinked features. First, participatory research is phenomenological.[1] Essentially, this means that the research focuses on what people think is true, rather than on what is actually true. What matters is the content of people's minds or consciousness, so that what is real is what people think is real. To explore the consciousness of other people, the researcher needs to adopt an exploratory frame of reference, to be open-minded, inclusive, and empathetic and to identify with the people in the study.

Second, participatory research is normative. Values are at the heart of how people see, think and feel about things, and it is not possible to lay these on one side. The researcher cannot maintain the fiction of being value-free or neutral. In recent years, particularly since the growth of organized sciences, what counts as knowledge has tended to become concentrated in fewer and fewer minds. Because 'knowledge is power', society has become further polarized between the powerful and the powerless, building on a related dichotomy between 'haves' and 'have nots' (Tandon, 1982). Researchers have to decide whether they wish to increase or to reduce the polarization. Neutrality is not an option because academic 'business as usual' will contribute to knowledge among the powerful, but not the powerless, and in the process will increase the gap, no matter what the researchers' intentions.

Third, participatory research is action based. The object is to raise consciousness so that people can begin to close the gap between their current and desired realities, and to change their situation in ways that they determine. The researcher acts as a change agent in the process.

WHAT IS PARTICIPATORY RESEARCH?

Participatory research involves people in generating knowledge about their own condition and how it can be changed. The methods of participatory research include collective research; critical reviews of history; valuing and applying folk culture; and oral and visual creation of knowledge (Cornwall, Guijt and Welbourn, 1994). The participatory research methods used here have been tried and tested in many fields (Chambers, 1997).

Participatory research has been developed in the Southern Hemisphere, though its origins were in the Bureau of Indian Affairs in the United States during the 1930s (Edwards, 1999). Popularized by the work of Freire (1970) in South America, participatory research in Africa was kick-started at a regional workshop in Tanzania in 1979 (Kassam and Kemal, 1982). In India, the Society for Participatory Research in Asia (PRIA) has built a solid array of methodologies and techniques (Tandon, 1997). Since then, techniques have become popular throughout the Southern Hemisphere and have spread to the North (Chambers, 1997).

COUNTERING CONVENTIONAL WISDOM

The participatory approach contrasts with the dominant scientific approach to social research in the Northern Hemisphere. Unlike participatory methodology, the scientific method separates the researcher from the material being researched.

Conventional science takes two main forms: deductive or inductive. In the deductive form, there is a progression from theory to hypothesis, to data collection, to analysis, to a decision on whether to reject the null hypothesis.[2] In the inductive form, there is standard sampling, pre-coded questions, coding and analysis, leading to a matrix of correlations, significance tests or other statistical procedures. In scientific terms the deductive form is commonly believed to be 'vastly superior' (Otterbein, 1990).

However, both of these scientific approaches are increasingly seen as inappropriate (Capra, 1982).[3] The scientific method in social theory derives from an era when belief in science and its applicability to all kinds of material was at its height. The final decades of the 20th century witnessed a disillusion with scientific certainty, in general, and in the field of social research, in particular. The scientific approach gives research an illusory rigour, as if it is dealing with fixed quantities that can be manipulated at will. However, by trying to coerce these unruly materials into pre-established categories, as if they are inert, analyses miss out the complexity, diversity, dynamics and unpredictability at work in every situation. Results display false precision.[4]

Moreover, scientific research of this kind reflects the preoccupations of the world's elites. Such research has, at its heart, a top-down and unequal view of the world that reproduces power imbalances in what passes for knowledge. Waddington (1977) described this accumulated knowledge of the world's elites as the 'conventional wisdom of the dominant group'. Since such wisdom is commonly flawed, Waddington felt no compunction in assigning the acronym COWDUNG to it.

The problem with COWDUNG is that top-down thought becomes top-down action, with the result that:

The idea of development stands today like a ruin in the intellectual landscape (Sachs, 1992).

Although this point is overstated, it is clear that many errors have flowed from well-meaning, top-down intervention. Writing a quarter of a century ago, John Turner (1975) criticized the pyramidal structures and centralizing technologies prevalent in housing developments across the world. Based on his work in low-income housing settlements in South America, he argued that local people knew best and argued for local control of developments. This would produce the requisite variety and 'equifinality' which are essential to freedom and genuine culture, and without which people's needs will never be met.

Equifinality is a vital concept here. This is a word used in systems theory to denote a multiplicity of routes to a single end.

Whereas pyramidal structures and centralizing technologies permit one route to a solution, cooperative structures and local autonomy permit many.

Participatory research functions much like equifinality. It allows many people to go along different routes towards a solution, finding their own pathways that are both creative and culturally appropriate. In this way, participatory research respects and builds on people's autonomy. Scientific research, by contrast, is based on the principle of heteronomy – the antonym of autonomy – so that local people have no control, with decisions and power vested in the hands of outside professionals.

Turner argued that:

Very deep changes of attitude have to take place before traditional politicians and 'unreconstructed' professionals can really serve ordinary people as they pretend.

Participatory research can help with this, and indeed the method is gaining acceptance among institutions such as the World Bank (Narayan, 2000). As with scientific research, not all participatory research has been of good quality. Nonetheless, at its best it can be an effective tool for development.

The main benefits of participatory research in development are as follows. First, experience to date shows that poor people are competent, and can do much of their own investigation, analysis and planning. Second, results from participatory research can illuminate courses for action, fusing together empirical and normative ideas into a change strategy. Third, the techniques bridge the gap between researcher and practitioner, as a corrective to the adage that 'thinkers don't do and doers don't think'. Fourth, the professional is recast as an enabler, rather than as a service provider or implementer, so that professionals are, in Tony Gibson's (1997) phrase, 'on tap, not on top'. Fifth, there is a strong educational element in participatory research that fosters the democratic spirit. Not only might the involvement of those directly concerned produce better solutions to their own problems than would outside professionals, but the process of participatory research allows participants to see changes that are taking place or that ought to take place and to become instrumental in effecting them for the general good. In Freire's phrase: 'people are made the agents of their own recuperation' (Freire, 1970). Finally, governments can respond to the kind of societies their citizens need and want, rather than telling them what they ought to want.

Such radical departures in thinking are bound to create resistance. As Robert Chambers (1997) has pointed out:

> *Professionalism, distance and power can combine with vested interests to offer spirited resistance to new insights.*

The current study is more than simply a contribution to a field that is growing in importance. It displays novel features intended to advance the field. Most previous research of this kind has been undertaken on a small scale, confined to a village or town. Translating it to an international level through a process of synthesis from the bottom up was a daring undertaking with uncertain prospects of success.

In sum, the research had five essential characteristics. First, it was inductive (building hypotheses from data, rather than data from hypotheses). Second, it was cross-cultural (seeing culture as a strength rather than as a difficulty to be incorporated in the data). Third, it was based on what Glaser and Strauss (1970) called grounded theory, which means that, as far as possible, the study was free from theoretical frameworks. Fourth, it used the methods of synthesis, building up pictures of society, based first on the views of people who are normally invisible to researchers – and debating the concerns they raise with a range of different people in society – and finishing with those who have most influence. Finally, the synthesis was a force for change at different levels: local, national, regional and global.

LIMITATIONS

All research methods have their limitations, and most social scientists are aware that the character of the results they obtain will partly be determined by the methods they use. In the context of the current study, it is important to acknowledge a number of limitations.

First, there is a limitation built into the term 'participatory'. In practice, professionals led the research and questions were formulated outside the communities researched. Nevertheless, the questions proved to be close to people's hearts, so that they were keen to answer them, suggesting that professional researchers used some measure of empathy to frame the questions in the first place.

Second, a few of the national partners were unaccustomed to a participatory ethos. This meant that they lacked the commitment to follow up the research to enable local people to take action – for example, by translating the results into local languages, circulating the results and setting aside time to discuss them. In part, this reflects the fact that the participatory approaches of civil society are still in their infancy, and (as we will see later) while many organizations across the world have added the prefix 'civil society' to their titles and names, changing organizations' cultures is much harder than changing their names. Many are still stuck in old-fashioned, top-down, elitist ways of conducting their business.

Third, by their nature, the primary data here are subjective. The research deals with the perceptions of respondents, and these may be at variance with the actual state of affairs. Where possible, secondary data in the form of academic studies, news reports and other material – which sets for itself a more or less rigorous standard of objectivity – has been used to cross-check these perceptions. Nevertheless, the reservation should be borne in mind.

Fourth, there were occasional concerns about the quality of reporting. Interpretations can only be as good as the reports on which they are based. In the current study, most of the reports were of a high standard, though a small minority required hands-on assistance from task force members (the professional team recruited from different parts of the Commonwealth to help implement the programme) to bring them up to scratch.

Fifth, the broad-ranging nature of the study has meant that analysis has concentrated on the similarities emerging across the national studies. For the purposes of synthesis, this is inevitable. However, such similarities, couched in general terms, might conceal differences in emphasis, even in meaning, when taken out of their native contexts. A general complaint, for instance, about the state of law and order in a country where civil strife is endemic is very different from a similar one in a country where standards of policing are felt anecdotally to have declined over a generation. In addition, although it is the common themes that have been the main focus of the study, consideration of the differences would be equally instructive. These tend to be localized; to an extent, they have been brought out in the national reports, to which the reader – in search of more concrete, more sharply focused diagnosis of particular social goods and ills – should turn.

Finally, the outputs of participatory research tend to be qualitative rather than quantitative. Conventional science has the merit of using quantities that can be manipulated using the highly advanced techniques of parametric statistics. At the present stage of development of participatory research, numbers are rarely obtained and usually fail to meet the criteria necessary even for non-parametric statistical treatment.

METHODOLOGY OF THE CURRENT STUDY

To find out what kind of society citizens wanted to live in and how government and citizens could create this, 10,000 citizens throughout the Commonwealth answered three basic questions:

1   What is your view of a 'good' society? To what extent does such a society exist today?

2   In order to build a 'good' society, what roles are best played by citizens and what roles are best played by state institutions and other sectors?

3   What would enable citizens to play their roles more effectively in the development of such a society in the future?

This framework, though precise, was not intended to be entirely prescriptive, and researchers had a certain leeway in order to take account of local conditions. It was often necessary to interpret questions and to conduct the interviews so that the respondents better understood them and could discuss them freely in the interviews. With this in mind, not only were the questions translated into the appropriate local language or dialect, in some cases – for example, in Guyana – they were rephrased according to the linguistic abilities of respondents. This was felt to be a necessary expedient in areas with low levels of formal education. In Zimbabwe, the research questions were slightly expanded to ensure that both researchers and respondents fully understood them.

IMPLEMENTING THE RESEARCH

The research questions were, for the most part, successfully implemented, and response rates within countries were high. Part of the reason for the success was that research teams invested time, energy and resources in making good connections with people. As far as possible, research teams reflected the ethnicity, gender, age, tribe and other characteristics of the different categories of citizens to be interviewed. Research teams went to great lengths to overcome the general suspicion of outsiders prevalent in some rural areas. In such cases, it was necessary to gain the confidence of people before they could be induced to participate. A technique that was used to good effect was to begin with community matters, adopting a general and conversational style. Once respondents gained confidence, they were able to talk along the same lines on a wider regional or national level. Overall, once they had learned what it was about, there was much enthusiasm for the project.

There were, however, some exceptions. Particular difficulty occurred in Namibia. Here, researchers encountered resistance because local people said that they had been overresearched, and that nothing had ever happened as a result of the research. In other countries, there were problems in areas where respondents felt themselves to be at risk of reprisals from the state if they voiced any criticism. Here, issues of confidentiality and confidence became paramount. To guarantee anonymity, no tape recorders were used, nor were participants photographed. In Trinidad and Tobago, there was so much suspicion that researchers had to give a full explanation of how the material would be used before people would consent. It is a testimony to the skill, persistence and tact of people in the research teams that the response rate was so high.

EXAMPLES OF METHODS USED

Box 2.1 and Box 2.2 provide two examples of how interviews were conducted. The first is an extract from the Trinidad and Tobago report.

In Fiji, the main method of research was through interviews. Box 2.2 presents extracts from the research about the fieldwork

CATEGORIZING RESPONDENTS

Citizens from different parts of society were consulted. The main focus was on ordinary citizens – for instance, indigenous peoples, rural labour, fisherfolk, slum dwellers, housewives, small businessmen, farmers, plantation labour, vendors, blue- and white-collar workers. In addition, people who were commonly excluded were included – young people, women, minorities, disabled people, refugees and the unemployed.

BOX 2.1 TRINIDAD AND TOBAGO CASE STUDY

In Trinidad and Tobago, individual and focus group interviews were used to collect primary data. Newspaper articles and letters to the editor were analysed. Some of the individuals who were selected to participate were community or national actors well known for their commentary or analysis of the socio-political and economic trends in society. Other individual interviews were solicited from passersby on the street. Individual interviews were conducted by at least two members of the team, one who acted as the main facilitator, while the other was charged with recording, either manually or electronically, and with paying attention for cues for follow-up questioning.

Groups were selected on the basis of their socio-political and economic location in society, on the guidelines of the project and on the social structure of this society, with its diverse ethnic and historical elements. The focus group interviews were conducted with a minimum of three members of the team: one main facilitator, a recorder and the third assisting with the questioning.

In discussion groups, every effort was made to provide a non-threatening, non-judgemental, safe space in which participants could share their views and experiences. A well-known local person was employed to recruit participants. We took into account the noise level in the area, and the possibility of personal and technological intrusions by non-participants. On all occasions, the seating arrangements of the group sessions were circular. Participants were given the assurance, before the start of the interview, that confidentiality would be guaranteed. All members of the team were introduced before the interview began and their functions in the project were explained. An explanation of the project was given to allay any fears that may have arisen concerning use of the material in the future.

Individuals in the planned interviews were solicited via telephone, email and letters. Particular attention was paid to the time of day and place for the interview in order to ensure that both interviewers and interviewees would be physically and mentally up to the task. Consent was sought from all participants before the interview for permission to audio/video tape, quote or photograph and, where possible, a letter of thanks followed the interview.

Interviewers shared their own experiences with interviewees with the express purpose of stimulating discussion, always mindful not to influence the perceptions shared by participants. Interviews ranged in duration from 45 minutes to two hours. Participants spoke freely about issues that they felt impacted on the research questions or issues they felt passionately about, with people whom they believed would empathize and not judge.

Questions were translated using the language most used by the participants. A sub-set of questions was asked to clarify the main question and participants were asked to develop the points they contributed so that the group, as well as the research, could benefit. For example, question 3 was: 'What would enable citizens to play their role in the development of society more effectively in the future?' Our translation was to pose the question personally by asking: 'What would you need in order to play the role you want to play to develop society more effectively or efficiently?'

The samples of ordinary people were supplemented with citizens' leaders. These were people who had taken a lead in public affairs and had gained some acceptance for their leadership from other citizens. The focus in interviews was on how their experiences could contribute to identifying factors that helped or hindered citizens' initiatives and leadership.

There were also interviews with people who occupied influential positions in society. These included political leaders, senior government officials, military leaders, scholars, professionals, media personalities, sports heroes, authors and playwrights, and business and NGO leaders.

The project covered all parts of the Commonwealth – small and large, island and mainland, rich and poor, East and West, North and South. The transitions at the turn of the millennium were affecting all countries of the Commonwealth – Belize and Britain, Nigeria and New Zealand, Pakistan and Papua New Guinea to name a few.

BOX 2.2 FIJI CASE STUDY

The target groups were urban and rural youths, urban and rural women and selected settlements. The interview also included the major church organizations, as well as a number of academics and other leaders falling in the category of interlocutors and coanalysts.

The young people were selected on the basis of their particular place in society. Their views, dreams, aspirations and current positions on national issues formed significant parts of the responses. Almost all of the Melanesian settlements visited had a sizeable number of young people who were early drop-outs from school, unemployed and disillusioned. It was not difficult to find this particular group as they existed in all settlements visited.

Other groups mentioned above, including churches, had direct relevance to the project given their distinct role in society. A few leaders and academics were also selected, not only because of their distinguished abilities but because of their knowledge of the target groups and their passion to see changes in the social system. The method used here was basically verbal interviews.

The method used to collect data varied in a few cases and situations. The first two interviews took an expanded version of the questions, which were found to be too lengthy. This was rectified by asking the key questions in their 'crude' form and allowing respondents to tell their story with minimum or only occasional interruptions when necessary for clarification or repetition of important phrases. Interviews conducted amongst young people needed constant encouragement in order to help them speak out their opinions; many tended to be shy, reserved and reluctant to converse. This problem was also experienced amongst women since speaking out one's mind is uncommon in traditional societies. Most interviews went smoothly with a lot of interaction and stimulating discussion.

Interviews were conducted on a one-to-one basis and in group sessions. Little difference could be identified between the two, although there were some reservations in group situations. On the whole, however, individuals and groups were equally fair in their responses. In the case of group interviews, discussions were encouraged in order to ensure maximum and quality responses. Most of the 50 interviews were conducted singly or in groups of two or three. There were four large group interviews in four settlements – namely, Wailoku, New Town, Caubati and Naviavia, with two youth groups: the Wailoku netball and Wailoku rugby teams. In most cases, discussions were lengthy and questions asked became very relevant as the research timing coincided with national election preparations.

Interviews with interlocutors, church leaders and academics took a different form. They were given the questions before interview schedules. Responses were made in summary form rather than the usual questions and response format. As expected, interviews flowed smoothly with deep responses. The use of media (newspaper) was frequent as it was the only form of literature resource available and was accessible to respondents, especially individuals from rural areas who provided the much needed information on the activities of the nation.

To achieve the necessary comprehensiveness and to admit some measure of comparability between countries, citizens were classed into one of four different groups in the study. The labels given to each of the four groups reflected their 'visibility' with regard to power in society.

Category 1: invisible citizens

'Invisible' is a term used in participatory research to indicate those persons who are typically not seen, heard, engaged, acknowledged, or empowered within any given society. Reasons for invisibility vary and are commonly based on a range of historical, economic, cultural or gender-based factors. Eighty-five per cent of all those interviewed were citizens not normally associated with national or regional politics or other forms of leadership – this group we called ordinary citizens.

Category 2: visible citizens

'Visible' in participatory research is used to denote people who are seen, heard and are engaged in society. The people identified under this category are typically leaders of particular groups and are linked in some way with invisible groups. To take an example from the study, when students in Bangladesh were interviewed as invisible citizens, student leaders were interviewed as visible citizens. Similarly, when urban women were interviewed as invisible citizens, women leaders from that area were interviewed as visible citizens. Ten per cent of those interviewed were community leaders.

Category 3: interlocutors

The term 'interlocutor' refers to people who are seen, heard, engaged, acknowledged and empowered in any society. They are, typically, prominent people in the voluntary, public and private sectors, social observers, politicians, journalists and others. By virtue of their position, interlocutors are able to address citizens' visions of a good society and can help or hinder the realization of these visions. In the study, such prominent citizens were asked to offer responses to the views and experiences of visible and invisible citizens, and to provide their distinctive inputs on these issues. Five per cent of the sample were influential leaders or decision-makers.

Category 4: coanalysts

These were people who had studied how societies work. They included academics, consultants, policy analysts, government observers and others.

CLUSTERING

People from different categories were clustered together into sub-groups with elements in common. The resulting clusters commonly comprised such categories as young people, women, indigenous peoples, professional workers, unskilled labourers, fishermen, copra workers, farmers, urban squatters, unemployed people and others. Table 2.1 illustrates how clustering was performed in the Indian study. Four (of a total of 19) clusters are shown for illustrative purposes.

The table relates types of clusters to numbers in each of the four citizen categories. In most countries, attempts were made to include a diversity of clusters in the project, as well as a diversity of people in each cluster. This enhanced the richness of the reports. The clusters were selected to follow the major social, economic and political developments in each country, and to balance urban and rural areas.

DEVELOPING A SYNTHESIS

The process of the study involved getting responses from invisible citizens first, and using results to inform discussions with visible citizens. These discussions were then used to inform discussions with interlocutors and, finally, with coanalysts. Figure 2.1 presents a very simple diagram of how this process was structured.

To show how this worked in practice, let us take the case of young people. The first step was to start with young people individually or in groups. The next stage was to take what the young people said to youth leaders and use this as a basis for discussion. The third stage was to take these two sets of findings and use them as a basis for discussion with government representatives or those responsible for developing youth programmes. As a final step, the results were discussed with a sociologist or specialist in youth behaviour.

Figure 2.1 *Pattern of discussions in the research*

THE INTERNATIONAL FRAMEWORK FOR THE RESEARCH

So far, we have described the research in the countries. Implementing the study across the Commonwealth involved a major process of strategic planning and resource mobilization, beginning with the political approval of the Commonwealth Heads of Government Meeting (CHOGM) in 1997.

To manage and implement the project, the Commonwealth Foundation and CIVICUS set up two key instruments: a task force and an Eminent Persons' Support Group. Both of these groups contained representatives from the five main areas of the Commonwealth: Africa, Asia, the Caribbean, the Pacific, and four developed countries of Aotearoa/New Zealand, Australia, Canada and the United Kingdom. Although the developed countries did not constitute a region in a geographical sense, they nevertheless had much in common.

Table 2.1 *Four of 19 clusters in India*

Serial no	Clusters	Description	No of Respondents			
			I	II	III	Total
1	Santhals in Bihar	Tribal Self-Rule in Jharkhand: The people of South Bihar have gone through a series of transformations in their cultural, socio-economic and religious status as a result of external influences due to industrial growth. They are traditionally nomads who gather forest products for their livelihood. A majority of them are also engaged in agriculture. They practise shifting cultivation and grow pulses and maize and cash crops, such as potatoes and tomatoes. Health-care facilities are poor in the area and there is a very low level of literacy. The local people, called Santhals, have their own system of governance, which is cherished by them. Ever since independence, the Santhals have demanded a separate home state in order to build their separate identity. But their demand has been rejected by all of the major political parties of the country. The Jharkhand Movement (the movement for a separate home state for the Jharkhandis) has enjoyed massive support from the people.	80	20	6	106
2	Hill tribals in Uttar Pradesh	Farmers in Jaunsari: The people of Jaunsari are economically backward. Agriculture is the primary occupation of the villagers. One of the unique features of this area is that the village forms the most important economic and social unit in the life of the people of Jaunsari. Due to great hardships, villagers have developed an intense community life, of which the village is the hub.	110	23	2	135

3	Tribals in Madhya Pradesh	Displacement of Tribals: The tribals in Gwalior are facing displacement, as their traditional habitats have been transferred to reserve forests; access to the forest has thus been denied. Forest authorities have justified their stand, claiming that the local inhabitants have been destroying the ecological balance of the forest.	70	20	7	97
4	Rural women in Orissa	Poor Women in Orissa: The problems faced by the poor women in Orissa are multifaceted. Almost any action having something to do with 'women' gets slotted into 'women's development'. Thus, although numerous programmes and actions continue, there has hardly been any improvement in the condition of women. The problems that women face in Orissa have never been addressed in a holistic manner. These problems include different forms of cultural oppression, feudalism, patriarchy and caste barriers.	95	20	7	122

In planning the project, the task force was guided by earlier Commonwealth Foundation work on the role and functions of NGOs. This focused on good practice and highlighted issues of accountability and transparency (Ball and Dunn, 1995). The task force judged that a broader view of civil society was needed, because it was vital to include citizens' contributions to civil society over and above their contribution to NGOs. In framing the questions for the study, the task force left the choice of appropriate agency to citizens, asking them to set out roles for government, for other players (such as NGOs, churches and businesses) and for themselves.

Once the overall research framework was settled, task force members were charged with the responsibility of identifying and training national partners to conduct the study within their regions. These were not necessarily professional research institutions. At least 34 of the national partners were NGOs or civil society organizations. Key tasks included: determining the size of samples of citizens to be interviewed; collecting case studies and published views of citizens from newspapers and other media outlets; identifying and working with academic support teams that could assist with secondary material reviews; collecting the primary material needed to answer the research questions; and writing national reports to inform the global and regional synthesis reports.

Two workshops were held in each of the five regions. The first workshops were directed at training national partners in the research methodology. Academics and professional researchers worked alongside task force members on the following themes: the importance and nature of the research; media and other source material collection; developing a bibliography; identification of samples; interviewing techniques; recording of interviews; analysis of interviews and secondary data; and report writing.

The second workshops were conducted after all of the material was collected and draft reports were ready. The purposes of the second workshops were to review the quality of national reports; to review the literature review reports commissioned from professionals; and to identify the common themes from the national reports that would be emphasized in the regional synthesis reports, which were later written by task force members. At both the first and second round of workshops, regional NGOs or interlocutors were invited to participate and comment.

The research tried to cover all 54 countries of the Commonwealth. In the end, national partners in 49 of those countries became involved in the project. Research reports were obtained from 47 countries. Five regional synthesis reports (covering Asia, Caribbean, the Pacific, Africa and the developed countries) were produced, together with an overall global synthesis report.

The global synthesis, *Citizens and Governance: Civil Society in the New Millennium*, was published by the Commonwealth Foundation and CIVICUS, and was presented to the CHOGM in Durban, South Africa, in November 1999. The regional syntheses were published by the Commonwealth Foundation and CIVICUS in 2001.

THE RISE OF CIVIL SOCIETY

Having set out the main aspects of the methodology, this section returns to the central topic of this inquiry: civil society.

Rarely has there been a concept in the development field that has grabbed people's attention so quickly and become so widely used in such a short space of time as the concept of civil society (Holloway, *Civil Society Toolbox*, 2000).

An alternative version might read: 'Rarely in the history of development can a term have progressed so quickly from obscurity to meaninglessness without even a nanosecond of coherence' (Knight and Hartnell, 2000).

Richard Holloway is right. Until ten years ago, the use of the term was confined to a few freedom fighters in oppressive regimes in Eastern Europe, South Africa and South America. An internet search today reveals more than 34,000 websites in which the term is used. Across the world, the prefix 'civil society' has suddenly become attached to centres, research institutions, foundations, university departments, government units, challenge funds, projects, conferences and much else. We even have the beginnings of an index from CIVICUS. Civil society is everywhere being strengthened, promoted and reinvented. This adds up to a huge industry.

But what is civil society? Is it an important political idea? A trendy jargon term for NGO activists? A job creation scheme for academics? A refuge for politicians who have run out of ideas? Or is it all of these?

It is striking that so much energy is being put into something that is so vague. Civil society is so plastic that it appeals right across the political spectrum. By endorsing civil society, people can commit to anything or to nothing. By the same token, there is room for everyone to be disappointed. One has only to look to the fate of the 'third way' in Germany. Because it attracts so much criticism for being vacuous, it is being quietly dropped. If the same fate befalls civil society, the notion of citizenship may fall off the political agenda, to be replaced with a new and unsympathetic set of ideas. A parallel might be the notion of state planning, which gripped the world's governments in the 1940s but was followed by disillusion and fell into disrepute, to be replaced by a new ideology in the 1970s – the free market.

Words, just like everything else, are subject to fashion, and if civil society is to continue occupying a prominent place in the intellectual landscape, it needs to stake its claim as something particular and useful on which people can agree. Many academics claim that civil society is a contested term. If so, what justification is there in continuing to use it unless we want to perpetuate confusion? Some social and political theorists such as Kumar (1993) have even gone so far as to question the usefulness of such a polymorphous concept as civil society. Either the term should be defined or dropped.

Part of the problem is that the term civil society has been used in many different ways in many different contexts at different points in the past. Most of the literature focuses on Western models of civil society, but even here there is little agreement on what constitutes civil society. A comprehensive study of the evolution of civil society in Western political thought by Dominique Colas (1997), a professor at the Paris Institute of Political Studies, reveals its different uses by media personnel, politicians, political theorists and anthropologists. Colas shows that civil society is a concept that has undergone, and is still undergoing, a process of evolution, serving the diverse social, economic, political and ideological needs of society. Colas suggests that most of the writing about civil society has come from philosophers or social theorists. Many trace the idea back to Aristotle, who equated civil society to the polis or state. Rousseau, Hobbes and John Locke considered civil society or the commonwealth as being in opposition to the state of nature. Hegel, on the other hand, was more concerned with the distinction between state and civil society, defining civil society as the sphere regulated by law and the professional corporations in which people might satisfy their needs through work. For him, civil society, far from being in antagonistic contradiction to the state, was closely related to it and could not exist without it. Karl Marx disagreed, restricting civil society to an economic entity devoid of political or juridical content.

There are a number of more recent studies of civil society that pursue these issues further (see, for example, Cohen and Arato, 1992; Gramsci, 1971; Gellner, 1994; Habermas, 1978; Hall, 1995; Seligman, 1992; Taylor, 1995). However, much academic writing suffers from being too theoretical, lacking reference to the real world. Conspicuously absent are historical studies that could put the theories to the test and begin to choose between them. In the absence of field studies that enable the empirical construction of the idea of civil society, it is hard to see how claim and counterclaim by academic theorists can be resolved, with the result that the debate about civil society has reached an impasse.

One key problem limiting the understanding of civil society is that it is largely invisible. Although civil society organizations in Eastern Europe have caught the public eye in recent years, civil society has been the bedrock of societies since time immemorial. Self-organizing in groups, clans, tribes or castes has been the driving force of culture, regulating relations between people and providing them with a sense of identity long before the rise of the nation state demanded that people identify with a particular country.

The customary informal local government that is exercised by chiefs and village and tribal councils in the Pacific Islands, for example, is still very real. Often, where the reach of central government is uncertain, these institutions exercise a more effective local control and are seen as doing so by local people themselves. Occasionally, 'jurisdictions' come into conflict, as each attempts to define its powers and responsibilities with respect to the other. In Dominica, the *koudmen* system lives on. This is a traditional form of agricultural cooperation that has survived the ravages of time and accounts for the vitality of civil society on the island. In South Asia, the village, with its customary institutions, has remained at the centre of rural life.

Civil society groups in these areas, therefore, have a long and continuous, although concealed, history, and have continued to serve as informal regulatory bodies at least at local level and, in many cases, as ginger groups agitating for political and economic consideration from the central government. Indeed, such civil society groupings (village and tribal councils, clan and kinship-based gatherings) have often provided social continuity at times of wider political turbulence when effective central authority has been either abrogated or completely wanting. Describing India under the Raj, Stern (1993) notes that: 'Prior to independence, the main role of baronial, princely and imperial regimes in the governance of the sub-continent's villages was to collect their taxes and, less dependably, to keep the peace.' Clearly, such groups antedate centralized forms of authority, and it has been suggested by some observers that civil society should properly be called the first sector, not the third sector (Tandon, 2000).

Such civil society groupings have frequently found themselves in opposition to the central power. This has been the case not merely in colonial times, but more recently where governments have been extremely reluctant to cede any of their authority. Indeed, they have often made use of the centralized state machinery in order to curtail the activities of civil society groups. The *Charter of Civil Society*, enacted in 1997 by some governments of the Caribbean, makes a number of high-sounding and praiseworthy assertions about respect for minority rights, responsible citizenship and participatory governance. However, this study reveals that little is known in the individual countries about the charter and its provisions. Moreover, some of those who have heard of it believe it to be no more than rhetoric, particularly in those countries where the efforts to establish a strong civil society would count as an implicit criticism of government policies and might incur wrath, prosecution or violence.

It is clear that civil society can flourish in adversity and in opposition to the established interests of state and capital. Take, for example, the kind of civil society that emerged in colonial states during the struggle for independence. Rebellious and overtly political, trade unions, labour movements, students unions and armed ethnic groups such as the *Mau Mau* (in Kenya) and *Maji Maji* (in Tanzania) spearheaded the struggle for self-rule in colonial states. Groups bearing similar characteristics championed the democratization process against the one-party regimes that followed independence. Clearly, this is a far cry from the role of civil society in the current consensus described in Chapter 1 and reveals the extent to which such a model is drawn from the perspective of the developed Northern Hemisphere countries.

Adversity was at the heart of civil society in the struggles for freedom in Central and Eastern Europe. During the 1970s and 1980s, democracy seekers in oppressive regimes in Central and Eastern Europe organized a space in which to express themselves and plan for change. They called this space civil society. In doing this, they drew on the ideas of the 18th-century Enlightenment. Philosophers such as John Locke described how civil society conferred natural rights for ordinary men and women in order to create communities for themselves without excessive interference from state or church.

The power of civil society showed itself in mass demonstrations in cities across Central and Eastern Europe in 1989, leading to the Velvet Revolutions. On 9 November 1989, amidst scenes of triumphant rejoicing, a mass of people committed an act of dramatic symbolism. They dismantled the Berlin Wall. A month later, in Romania, 100,000 people in Timisoara faced down the armed guards of the Ceausescu regime, and 111 of them gave their lives to bring down communism's most repressive state. In Africa, dictatorial regimes in Malawi, Benin, the former Zaire, Zambia and South Africa gave in to the pressure from opposition groups backed by civil society organizations.

Stimulated by these developments in the East and the South, the idea of civil society caught on quickly in the West and the North. By the mid 1990s, there was much literature reminding us of our mutual responsibilities as citizens. Amitai Etzioni (1995) put forward 'communitarianism', Robert Putnam (1993; 1995) stressed the importance of 'social capital', Francis Fukuyama (1995) noted the value of 'trust', David Selbourne (1994) the virtues of 'duty', and a variety of writers analysed different forms of 'civil society' (Knight and Stokes, 1996).

The current success of the idea of civil society is due, in part, to the fall of secular ideology caused by the collapse of communism and its perceived role in bringing about that collapse, and the failure of mere capitalism to supply an alternative that will at once have moral weight, inspire loyalty and satisfy social needs. Civil society has provided a replacement ideology. At its best, it can provide one of the building blocks for a good society that values people, regardless of age, gender, race, disability or other aspects of social background. Civil society can create a capacity for leadership within communities which, if harnessed and nurtured, could transform democracy and reshape the balance of power in favour of greater social inclusion, justice, dignity, equality of opportunity and respect. Civil society might balance the excesses of the market, creating 'social capital' – the glue that binds people together in relationships – and might add meaning to people's lives over and above their role as economic producers or consumers.

However, civil society, in practice, at times runs counter to the idealized view that it is an element of democratic and participatory governance. It can be the product of extremely conservative and hierarchical societies who institutionalize grave inequalities, the more so because, in those societies where autochthonous culture has been driven underground by foreign overlordship, they are self-conscious custodians of tradition. These fora can often be the preserve of the more powerful or influential families and be dominated by clientage and deference, rather than by collective decision-making. The best and worst of civil society was found in Kosovo before the war, where impressive elements of self-help and self-organization were combined with amoral familism and terrorist activity (Knight, 1999).

It is clear from this brief review that civil society is a highly ambiguous social construct that can be used in a variety of ways. The most common uses are as follows:

- anything that is not government;
- the sphere of interaction between the state and the market;
- NGOs: variously called voluntary organizations, charities, non-profits, third-sector organizations and civil society organizations;
- community organizations: variously called civil society organizations, citizens' organizations, people's organizations,

village associations, networks of kith and kin, women's groups and clans;

- societies and clubs: groups that express a variety of interests, from choral societies to pigeon clubs;
- partnership organizations: hybrids in various blends of public, private, voluntary and community organizations that regenerate the economy or the environment;
- social movements: coalitions or broad-based organizations that form a bulwark against global capitalism and press forward issues relating to consumers, women, land, race and the environment;
- citizen action: what citizens do to improve their living and working conditions;
- the press and media, the freedom of which is a vital part of civil society;
- the internet: a vehicle for mass communication, leading to citizen action and leaderless demonstrations in various cities across the globe following the meeting of the World Trade Organization in Seattle in 1999
- café society: dissidents creating space in which to talk to one another;
- politeness: situations where people say 'please' and 'thank you'.

Given this plethora of uses, it is hardly surprising that the attempt to come up with a satisfactory definition of civil society has encountered difficulties. Even the attempt to define civil society organizations, arguably a less daunting task, has tended to fall at one of two hurdles in either defining the term too narrowly or so inclusively as to render it meaningless. The absurd frequency with which the question: 'What about the Ku Klux Klan? Isn't it part of civil society?' still arises, and the (theoretical rather than practical) perplexity it continues to create is symptomatic of the failure to define civil society in descriptive terms.

With so many different uses in evidence, one might perhaps conclude that civil society is a *portmanteau* term used to point to a vague sphere of relationships. Under this interpretation, civil society acts to unite people around a common cause so that they can talk to one another.

And what do they talk about? A content analysis of conferences on civil society would reveal that what they talk about is progress. They talk about how to improve society; how to reduce poverty; how to increase democracy; and how to create unity in the struggle for these goods. Civil society functions in this way as a metaphor for 'hope for a better world'.

There is nothing wrong with this. Indeed, our view is that it is impossible to separate the idea of civil society from the idea of progress towards a better world. This argument brings civil society right back to its 18th-century origins. The Enlightenment, particularly in Scotland, saw the need to replace societies based on fixed, hierarchical relationships of a social and economic character, military power and religious intolerance with societies based on commercialism and civil (as opposed to religious or military) society. In addition to the respect gained through transactions based on equality – that is, the ability to trade in the market – the recognition of what people did in the public sphere for the common good was seen as an essential component of the transition from feudalism to capitalism (Hunt, 1999). It is striking that the idea of civil society has emerged again at a point of great transition. This time, as the world shifts from authoritarian regimes to liberal democracies, civil society is seen as an essential element of social development, counterpoised to the state and the market economy.

What has gone wrong in our understanding of civil society is that much of the recent literature has separated it from the idea of progress in transition. Instead, it has tended to conceive of civil society as a coefficient of organizations and sectors (Salamon and Anheier, 1994). When this approach is combined with the domination of the field of study by economists and the academic publishing convention of peer review, among a restricted range of contemporary scholars, it tends to produce a narrowness of view that we earlier described as the 'conventional wisdom of the dominant group'.

Such conventional wisdom about civil society is limited and distorted because it relies on top-down research methods that locate organizations as the primary unit of analysis, largely because organizations, or at least registered organizations, are easy to recognize.

As we will see later in this book, results from this study suggest that citizens, including many who come from hitherto excluded and marginalized sections of our societies, define civil society as *individual and collective action towards the common public good*.

The first part of this definition suggests that the unit of analysis of civil society should be individual and collective action. It is therefore not just the province of organizational behaviour to conform to some standard of *not* being government or business. Instead, such individual and collective action includes what government officials and business entrepreneurs do for the public good in their communities and neighbourhoods. This connects with the agenda of global corporate citizenship (that is to say, that companies can work individually and collectively for the common public good) and with standards of good governance in the public sphere (government as an individual stakeholder in collective decision-making and action).

The second part of the definition suggests a further unit of analysis – namely, the common public good. The literature on civil society has tended to run a mile from such ideas because it is easier to count and classify organizations than it is to wrestle with the messy and turbulent world of aspirations and values. But this is *the big one*, and it is the one from which we should not run away. We believe that it is vital to get to grips with normative ideas – otherwise there will be no development towards the common good.

Our view is that it is impossible to separate civil society from aspirations and values. Is the Ku Klux Klan part of civil society because it is a voluntary non-profit organization with a membership structure and a dues base, and which pursues its purposes vigorously and with passion? No, of course it is not. It fails on the criterion of common public good because it preaches a philosophy of separation, supremacy and sectarianism.

Critics will suggest that the idea of a common public good is a contested one. We agree. It involves values and, by definition, values are contestable. We argue, however, that the term civil society need not be contested. Instead of arguing about what is and is not included in civil society, we should be arguing about what is and is not included in the notion of the common public good.

There is probably more agreement than we think. Kumi Naidoo (2000), Secretary General of CIVICUS, has made a plea for work on values, suggesting that previous work – for instance, the *Universal Declaration of Human Rights* – gave a precedent for how this could be done.

We suggest that civil society has a usefulness only if it attempts to achieve a better world. In our definition, civil society is more than a metaphor; it is individual and collective action, sometimes through NGOs and sometimes not, in pursuit of the common public good.

The appeal of this definition is that we know we have not yet achieved it; civil society is something for which we must continue to strive. In striving, there is the prospect of finding some unity about how to achieve the common public good.

Giving citizens pride of place is vital to civil society. As this chapter has attempted to show, it is more than the collection and sum total of formal, institutional NGOs. Rather, it is about what citizens do, individually and collectively, to meet their needs and to advance their own interests, while also advancing the general human condition. Civil society is about *association*, both formal and informal, with others – to do things which need to be done and which are not, or cannot be, done by the state or by the market. And it is therefore about *connection* – between citizens and their institutions of government, and between citizens and their organizations and associations. The voices of citizens need to be at the centre, and it is to this topic that we now turn.

CHAPTER 3

A Good Society

A good society is like building a house together
(homeless man in Belize)

INTRODUCTION

In this chapter, we give citizens' views of what constitutes a good society. We compare the results of theoretical conceptions of a good society described in Chapter 1 with the empirical results from the study.

We will see that the citizens in the study had a strong sense of what constitutes a good society. Furthermore, there was some measure of agreement about the ingredients of a good society; this was more down to earth and practical than the theories of academics. Citizens seek a new blend of society, based on the best of modernity and the best of tradition.

As we saw from Chapter 2, the research asked open-ended questions so that citizens would feel free to respond in ways that were meaningful for them. This produced a vast amount of data. For the researcher, such richness is both rewarding and problematic. What the data gain in authenticity by not being forced into pre-coded categories may be lost unless they are interpreted carefully. Analysing the results requires careful listening to catch the subtle nuances of all the different voices. Researchers have to find where voices agree and disagree. In this chapter we look, firstly, at what the different voices have in common and later how they differ.

A MODEL

Although ideas about a good society were expressed in different ways, there was an impressive consistency about the data that enabled the construction of a 'good society' model that was grounded empirically in the views of the citizens.

Needless to say, all models oversimplify. The current model has the merit of being faithful to the data and testable by subsequent research. Above all, it yields an ideal that people can mull over, argue about and act upon if they wish.

THREE BASIC COMPONENTS

In the views of citizens, a good society boils down to three components. The first component relates to the fulfilment of the *basic needs* of citizens. The second component concerns *association* with other people. The third component is about *participation* in the governance of society.

The three components are linked. Each provides an essential foundation for the next. If the foundation is absent or deficient, the next layer will be insecure. Indeed, it is only when one layer is built that people can even begin to include the next in their dreams and expectations of a good society. The model is hierarchical, as is depicted in Figure 3.1.

BASIC NEEDS

Three kinds of basic need emerged from the study as being important for citizens. The first was *economic security*; the second was services; and the third was *physical security and peace*.

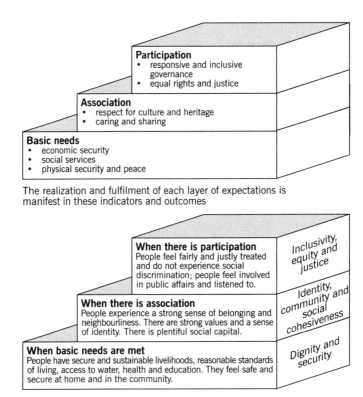

Figure 3.1 *The three components of a good society*

Economic security

A crucial basic need was economic security. This idea found expression in different ways. For farmers in Kenya, it meant the security of markets for farm produce. For women in Belize, it meant access to credit and technology. For young people in New Zealand, it meant employment and jobs. For tribal people in India, it meant access to forests and natural resources. Citizens wanted a society where economic security was a reality for all, whatever the social or cultural context:

> *Water for irrigation... Loans for meeting needs during famine... Employment for my children* (tribal elder in Bihar, India).

It is such a shame when you leave school with all your passes and cannot find work (a young man in Dominica).

I am earning less [than enough] to provide for my family's food, housing, clothing, education (a self-employed man in Ghana).

The San have nothing and if you have nothing what future can you imagine? (a citizen in Namibia).

If every family can have a plantation of bananas, yams, taamu, cocoa and copra, there will be no problem of food and living (a Samoan farmer).

For almost everyone, economic security was associated with the dignity of meaningful work. The availability of welfare, 'dole' or subsidy was not enough; it was, by a long way, second best. A young Maori woman in Aotearoa/New Zealand put it succinctly:

The government expects us to walk along a very narrow bridge, just surviving. Being dependent on the benefit grinds down the spirit.

Services

The second kind of basic need was the provision of adequate services. These included access to food, water, shelter, education, sanitation and health. Such items were a necessary condition for a decent and dignified life:

We should have a home – that is my dream. My life has passed without it but my children should not pass their lives like this (a woman pavement dweller in Mumbai, India).

The availability of drinking water and sanitation facilities was vital:

... where villages enjoy the privilege and access to good quality water... Even in drought conditions (a Fijian farmer).

So, too, was the availability of a functioning physical infrastructure (roads, electricity, markets, transport, etc):

Let's have sites and shelters so that we can start small businesses here near our land (a woman from rural South Africa).

Education was a priority. Despite improved literacy and increased school enrolments in many countries of the Commonwealth, numerous citizens were concerned about the quality and relevance of education and its availability to all children:

An education system...that suits the current situation... Incorporating good values and economic development (a Sinhalese woman in rural Sri Lanka).

We are sick of looking after animals, going hungry and being beaten up all the time. We have the right to education, food and freedom (a boy in Lesotho).

Citizens suggested that the availability of services should be for *all*, and not just for *some*. Otherwise, the result would be inequality. This would result in social exclusion, which would, in turn, lead to a downturn in people's sense of physical security.

Physical security and peace

Safety was the third kind of basic need:

A good society is disturbed when men use alcohol and abuse women and children (an older woman in Malawi).

A society where a woman can travel alone is good (a rural woman in Sri Lanka).

We need the protection of the leaders and officers who are there to look after the interests of the people (a teenage Amerindian girl in Guyana).

On pay day, we particularly feel insecure as our money is often taken away by the local musclemen and landlords (a women's group in Bangladesh).

Citizens said that a good society was free from war, crime, violence, drugs, killings and suicides. Physical attacks by hooligans in Fiji, gang wars in the slums of South Africa and racial hatred attacks in Australia were condemned by citizens, just as they condemned drug crimes in Jamaica, war in Sri Lanka and political violence in Mozambique.

I hope we can live in a peaceful society (a Malaysian taxi driver).

If there is no peace there is no freedom (a woman in Sri Lanka).

...a society where there are no gangs and no alcohol (a Mayan teenager in Belize).

People are frightened to go out in the evening (a citizen in the UK).

The importance of basic needs

These findings about basic needs may appear to state the obvious. All people have certain basic needs without which life would be impossible. Such life-sustaining basic human needs include food, shelter, health and protection (Lisk, 1983; Gosh, 1984). When any of these is absent or in critically short supply, we may state without reservation that a condition of 'absolute underdevelopment' exists (Todaro, 1991). A necessary condition of the quality of life in these circumstances is economic development. Without improvement in the economic life of a community, the realization of human potential is impossible. One clearly has to 'have enough in order to be more' (Goulet, 1971).

The importance of basic needs in international development has been recognized for many years. As long ago as 1980, the OECD published an analytical bibliography listing 250 pages of titles on the subject of basic needs (Garcia-Bonza, 1980). The literature suggests that eliminating absolute poverty, raising per-capita incomes, providing greater employment opportunities and lessening income inequalities are necessary conditions for development (International Labour Organization, 1976).

Although these findings about basic needs are obvious to citizens, they have not always been obvious to the world's elite. At the time of colonial independence, many leaders promised rapid improvement in the quality of life. They nurtured the hope of economic development, more education, expanded health facilities and a better standard of living (Anyang Nyongo, 1983). However, in most independent countries, governments withdrew from the responsibility of meeting citizens' basic needs. They passed the responsibility on to municipalities or private enterprises, making access dependent upon the ability to pay and depriving functionaries of job security. The early version of the 'Washington consensus' tended to classify the basic needs approach as philanthropy, a category of expenditure that was seen as wasteful because it diverted resources that were urgently required for growth (Raffer and Singer, 1996). Rather than meeting basic needs, development efforts focused on structural adjustment programmes whose leitmotif was 'aid to support economic-stabilization policy reforms and adjustments to public expenditure priorities' (OECD, 1994). Such measures were meant to help the poor by a process of 'trickle down', so that wealth created at the top of a society would flow downwards to those at the bottom. However, this approach was flawed because structural adjustment programmes have tended to polarize incomes and wealth so that the world's elite gained at the expense of the poor (Cornea et al, 1996). Structural adjustment programmes often survived despite these negative effects, in part because ruling elites in the South gained from the trickle-down theory of economic development and had little interest in helping the poor (Raffer and Singer, 1996).

Development professionals who wanted to revive the basic needs approach had to use an economic rather than a social argument. The argument suggested that, by fulfilling the basic needs of nutrition, health and education, labour would be more efficient and more productive. Meeting basic needs was, therefore, a means to an end and not an end in itself (Streeten, 1993). As we saw in Chapter 1, there is now more emphasis on poverty reduction as a goal in itself. Alex Wilks, coordinator of the Bretton Woods Project – which monitors the World Bank and IMF on behalf of NGOs – has suggested that, as one indicator of this, the *World Development Report 2000–2001* is a much more balanced and useful contribution to policy debates than many of the World Bank's previous publications (Wilks, 2000).

ASSOCIATION

The next level up from basic needs in the model was association. This had two main components: firstly, *respect for culture and heritage* and, secondly, *caring and sharing in the community*. What was at stake here was a culture of 'togetherness'.

Respect for culture and heritage

Culture and heritage are what people express – through music, art, craft, dance, ceremony, ritual, dress, food, meetings or language –

as part of their collective identity and purpose. Such expression affirms and reinforces relationships of many kinds, including those of families, tribes, neighourhoods and social networks. Culture and heritage bestow social norms and ethics, whether based on religious or spiritual beliefs, or temporal virtues, such as integrity, honesty, openness, cooperation and respect. Respect for such culture and heritage is a vital part of what people jointly own and share over time. After meeting basic needs, culture appears to be the bedrock of people's lives:

> *Pacific communal systems work, provide for basic needs and senses of identity and belonging. The individual does not exist except as part of a group in the Pacific* (a woman in the Pacific).

> *There should be room for old meeting places and water catchment sheds* (an elder from Nauru).

> *In a good society, men respect women, children respect elders, traditional values are respected* (a woman in Malawi).

Several citizens remembered the 'good old days'. But they were not merely talking about a return to traditional rigidities and hierarchies or cultural ethnocentrism. What they wanted was a balance between traditional and modern systems and structures:

> *The Fasamoa has good elements but the attitudes of Matai (traditional chiefs) need to change for greater tolerance* (a youth in Samoa).

The modernization of culture was important because of the need to include women and youth, who were commonly left out of many traditional cultures and systems.

Caring and sharing

The second component of association was caring and sharing: the values of fellowship, generosity of spirit, mutual help, solidarity and support. Maori in New Zealand call it *aroha* (love, respect and acknowledgement). For Gurus in India it is *sangat* (good company). South Africans talk about *ubuntu* (a humane society). In Dominica, the expression used is *koudmen* (cooperation to help each other in performing tasks).

> *A society which shares and cares for human life, where young greet the old and help them to do their chores and cross the street to fetch water, if needs be* (an older woman in Dominica).

> *People need to feel good about themselves... Have a feeling of pride and identification with the community* (a Maori woman leader in Aotearoa/New Zealand).

> *I think it is helping one another* (a woman in the UK).

> *I have recently settled here...my Indian neighbours have faith in us. They look after our house when we go out. They park their cars in our compound for us to look after. We look after their home. When they have no water we give from ours. Since we came, there has been a decrease in crime. We share extra crops. This kind of relationship has to be extended to other societies* (an indigenous Fijian).

> *We go to serve in a community; people come to help. We share with them about care and love* (a youth leader in Malaysia).

> *Our youth is missing love and communication* (a grandmother in the Seychelles).

I get help from my fellow farmers (a farmer in Jamaica).

We have a cooperative store in the village and a bakery run by women. There are about ten people baking and looking after the shop. We anticipate [employing] another ten if the loan is approved by the bank (a citizen in Fiji).

The importance of association

Association has a long pedigree in social science literature, going back at least to de Tocqueville's visit to America in 1831 (de Tocqueville, 1988). The idea of association has spawned many related concepts: attachment, community, belonging, trust, exchange, mutual aid, reciprocity, social networks, good neighbours, generosity and social capital. Towards the end of the 19th century, Durkheim stressed the importance of solidarity in social relationships (Durkheim, 1893). In the 1930s, the Chicago Ecologist School of Sociology used the theory of differential association to explain crime, believing that 'birds of a feather would flock together' (Sutherland and Cressey, 1970). In the 1940s, John Bowlby developed attachment theory, which stressed the importance of social bonds in developing balanced and integrated personalities (Bowlby, 1956). Bowlby (1946) argued, following de Tocqueville, that processes of association were vital for the development of democratic societies. Others have suggested that association is important for moral development (Titmuss, 1970), self-help (Wann, 1995), mutual aid (Beveridge, 1948), parenting (Winnicott, 1964) and many other factors that contribute to a secure society (Kramer and Roberts, 1996).

Association is what binds us in relationship to one another. A current vogue term for this is social capital. Despite its fashionable status, the term social capital was first used more than 80 years ago:

In the use of the phrase 'social capital'...we do not refer to real estate or to personal property or to cash, but rather to

that in life which tends to make those tangible substances
count for most in the daily lives of people: namely goodwill,
fellowship, sympathy and social intercourse among the
individuals and families who make up a social unit... If a
person comes into contact with his neighbours, there will
be an accumulation of social capital, which may
immediately satisfy his social needs and which may bear a
social potentiality sufficient for the substantial
improvement of life in the whole community... An
accumulation of community social capital [may be] effected
by means of public entertainments, picnics and a variety of
other community gatherings (Hanifan, 1920).

The modern debate about this stems from the work of two
Americans – the sociologist James Coleman, writing in the 1980s,
and the political scientist Robert Putnam, writing in the 1990s –
and Frenchman Pierre Bourdieu, again writing in the 1990s. It is
striking that social capital is an economic metaphor, and part of its
popularity may be due to the fact that, like basic needs, it is treated
as a precondition of economic growth (Putnam, 1993).

Coleman (1990) suggests that social capital is not a single entity
and is to be found in the relationships between people. What really
matters is its function, so that like other forms of capital, social
capital is productive, making certain jobs 'doable' that would not
have been done without it. On this model, a group whose members
manifest trustworthiness and who place extensive trust in one
another will be able to accomplish more than a comparable group
lacking that trustworthiness. Putnam (1993) suggests that 'social
capital...refers to features of social organization, such as trust,
norms and networks, that can improve the efficiency of society by
facilitating coordinated actions'. Bourdieu (1992) considers social
capital to be 'the sum of resources, actual or virtual, that accrue to
an individual or group by virtue of possessing a durable network of
more or less institutionalized relationships of mutual acquaintance
and recognition'.

Differences between academic definitions are small and inconsequential. At the heart of all of them is the importance of people coming together in association. What is notably absent from the current academic debate is the fact that the processes of building social capital through association are difficult. Part of the reason is that such processes inevitably contain elements of both cooperation and conflict. In the classic work on this subject, Tuckman (1965) reviewed a number of studies and found that the process of association in small groups typically advanced through four stages: forming, storming, norming and performing. The storming stage is characterized by conflict, with rebellions against leaders, battles between sub-groups, polarized opinions, resistance to control and conflicts over intimacy acting as visible signs of the stage. Studies suggest that association is a complex issue and that, for all their romantic associations, communities are far from universally friendly places in which to live (Bulmer, 1986).

Community studies reached their apotheosis in the 1960s and, in recent times, have tended to fall off the research agenda of university departments (Knight, 1999). The consequence is that there is a shortage of recent credible ecological studies on how ordinary communities behave and solve problems. Much of the recent academic literature is both abstruse and prosaic.

A notable exception is a particularly erudite study of the processes of building social capital in the poor areas of Karachi by Kenneth and Nora Fernandes (1997). The study consists of a series of stories told by squatters about their efforts to work with one another in order to provide facilities for themselves. In Karachi, there are about 650 *katchi abadis*. These are areas of settlement where the city's migrants (whose population has grown from half a million in 1947 to today's ten million) have squatted on land and built housing without regard for the legal ownership of the land. The squatters' greatest need is for water and sanitation, but they also have to provide work for themselves and education for their children. Stories show a record of achievement and suggest that people are able to form *tanzeems* (informal associations), which develop projects to sustain individuals in the most difficult of circumstances. At the same time, the stories reveal hard work, slow progress, difficulties in reaching decisions, splits and conflicts, and personal resentments – indeed, all the facets of collective human endeavour revealed in its glorious and gruesome multiplicity. Somehow, the human spirit wins out, and the results are sometimes noble. In creating a school, one participant noted: 'We did not have much experience of working together. However, we were all deeply interested in promoting education.' Another said of the school: 'In 1947, when we migrated to East Pakistan, all our wealth was looted. The same thing happened in 1970. One asset that they could not take away from us now is our education.'

What is vital to note about the Pakistan example is that these networks and associations are informal. A study in Uganda noted that such informal networks and associations of poor people are common in rural areas. In the absence of connections to state and resources, these associations become critical for survival – they become poor people's lifelines (Ministry of Finance, 1999).

Data in the current study confirm the importance of social capital. Although most citizens were unfamiliar with the jargon of political or social scientists, they well understood the importance of bonds between themselves and others, and many used them every day to achieve what they wanted, or needed, to do.

PARTICIPATION

The highest level in the model was participation. There were two aspects to this: *equal rights and justice*, and *responsive and inclusive governance*.

Equal rights and justice

The concept of equal rights and justice includes a number of related ideas, including respect for the rule of law, together with various freedoms – most notably, speech, information, association and assembly.

> *A good society upholds the rule of law and human rights for all its people* (a villager from Zimbabwe).

It also implies equality before the law and the absence of discrimination:

> *All people should be treated equally; there should not be rulings for the poor and rulings for the rich* (a primary school teacher in rural Kenya).

> *A good society is one that makes laws to protect everybody…a society where everybody – the poor, the middle class and the rich – get the same rights* (a fisherman in Jamaica).

This absence of discrimination should extend to every citizen – irrespective of origin, gender, class, culture or political and religious beliefs. The Caribs in Dominica, for example, want no more than other individuals; they just want no *differentiation* from others. A citizen in Trinidad and Tobago talked of the need for a 'level playing field for all'; while in Nauru, another asserted: 'We all demand to be treated equally as we are all created equal in the eyes of the Creator, God Almighty.' In Malaysia, a plantation worker complained that 'one race gets all'; and in Uganda, a farmer said: 'you get loans and seeds…if you belong to the party'.

> *A good society is one that's fair to all groups, where there is tolerance for all races… [it] supports equality of citizens* (a female youth leader in Guyana).

Equal rights and justice should include equal rights, as well as respect and dignity, for women. Poor working women in

Bangladesh, indigenous communities of Samoa in the Pacific, youngsters in Guyana and farmers in Uganda all emphasized the dream of a good society where women have equal rights and status:

The reality is that women still have little opportunity to participate in decision-making processes at all levels of the society (a Tongan woman senior government official).

I feel confined within strict boundaries in society (a film actress from Sri Lanka).

Concern for equal rights and social justice implies the right to self-determination of indigenous peoples, such as the Maori in New Zealand, tribal peoples in India and the Iban and Kayans of Sarawak in Malaysia. It further implies respect for the rights of other minorities, such as ethnic, religious, racial or linguistic groups.

Responsive and inclusive governance

The second component of participation was responsive and inclusive governance, so that citizens can participate in the public sphere and make their own contribution towards the common good.

Responsive and inclusive governance means being heard and consulted on a regular and continuing basis, not merely at election time. It means more than a vote; it means involvement in decision- and policy-making by public agencies and officials:

The government cannot do without its subjects; if they are not carrying them along, then things will go wrong (a ward leader in rural Nigeria).

During elections, they [the politicians] visit us individually to pocket maximum votes, but afterwards they evade us and we feel evil-smelling. First they hug us and later our sweat and grime repels them (a peasant from Baluchistan, Pakistan).

Politics is for upliftment [of others], not for personal gain. Politics should be what it ought to be (a group of Garifuna women in Belize).

People with dissenting political views are seen as opponents of government and their views not considered, even if they are in the interests of the country (a butcher in Ghana).

Usually the government promises a lot of things, but when you approach them with a problem, they can't help you (a construction worker in Malaysia).

We want God-fearing leaders who will clean our tears (a farmer in Kenya).

If government trusted the private sector, it could play a much greater role in education and training and entrepreneur development (a senior manager in a private company in Mauritius).

Sarkar [the government] is far away from us and the government officials do not visit our village; when we go to meet them, they refuse to meet us. It is so distant from us, how can it work for our benefits and address our needs? (a member of a nomadic tribe in India).

Responsive and inclusive governance involves the eradication of corruption, favouritism, nepotism, apathy, neglect, red tape and self-serving political leaders and public officials. It means a democracy that works for all.

The importance of participation

Like basic needs and association, citizens' desires for participation are not new. The earliest model we have of this is of ancient Greece, captured in Aristotle's polis, in which free men engaged in direct democracy. The idea of citizen participation came to prominence again during the 18th-century Enlightenment, when writers such as Adam Ferguson, John Locke and Adam Smith suggested that the twin pillars of civil society and commercialism would free society from the shackles of serfdom, superstition and subservience (Hunt, 1999).

In modern times, the Third World Community Development Movement saw the limitations of classical representative democracy (Schumpeter, 1942) and espoused the virtues of neighbourhood democracy (Dahl and Tufts, 1973). A key part of this was populist theory in which 'virtue resides in the simplest people who are in the overwhelming majority in their collective traditions' (Wiles, 1969). Neighbourhood democracy and populist theory display a range of different approaches, though common to all of them is the idea that ordinary folk are badly treated (Stewart, 1969).

Although populist theory owes much to the self-organizing perspective that derives from the ideas of 19th-century anarchists such as Peter Kropotkin, and from the practice of political activists such as Mahatma Gandhi, many of the first active proponents of participatory approaches were missionaries and colonists (Mayo, 1975). Indeed, the British Colonial Office set up an Advisory Committee on Native Education and its 1944 report, *Mass Education in the Colonies*, promoted self-help as a means of delivering agriculture, health and social services (Midgely, 1986). By the 1950s, the idea of community development figured prominently in United Nations documents and there was a growth of 'how-to-do-it' manuals (Batten, 1962). Kuenstler (1960) provided academic recognition of the community development approach.

The concept of community development was imported into the United States and later the United Kingdom. In 1960s America, there was a 'war on poverty'. The leitmotif of the approach, set out

Table 3.1 *Arnstein's ladder of participation*

Rung	Type of participation	Strategy
8	Citizen control	Power-sharing
7	Delegate power	
6	Partnership	
5	Placation	Degrees
4	Consultation	of
3	Informing	tokenism
2	Therapy	Non-participation
1	Manipulation	

in the 1964 Economic Opportunity Act, was 'maximum feasible participation'. The theory was that participation would create opportunity, which would reduce poverty, which would in turn lead to the Great Society. Emblematic of this new mood were measures to bring about 'new careers for the poor' (Pearl and Weissman, 1965).

How successful were the programmes? A useful tool to measure citizen participation was devised by Arnstein (1969). Her ladder of participation has eight rungs, as shown in Table 3.1.

Arnstein argues that the essence of authentic participation is power-sharing. It follows that participation is only authentic at the top three levels of the ladder.

Joan Higgins has shown that most participation in the US and UK poverty programmes of the 1960s took place on the lower rungs of the ladder (Higgins, 1980). One exception occurred during the early days of the US Community Action Programme. Here, community groups could spend money as they saw fit and could control programme content. However, these powers were gradually clawed back by the authorities. Too often, Higgins points out, government institutions wanted cooption, not liberation. She concludes: 'the portrayal of mass participation in the programmes is largely mythical' and suggests that the programmes were a 'cruel hoax'.

As participation declined in the West, a similar fate occurred in the East and the South. In some countries, expectations were too high, leaving too much room for disappointment, even among those who were actively involved (Smillie, 1995). In other countries, corruption, poor administration and inefficiency meant that resources designed to foster the participation of ordinary people never reached them (Midgely, 1986). The main beneficiaries of programmes tended to be the officials running them (Hancock, 1989). The result was that, during the 1970s, the issue of participation went into decline and was replaced by an emphasis on growth, transfer of capital industry, heavy industry and economic modernization. In Africa, many governments continued to use the rhetoric of participation, yet failed to provide resources to make this a reality; meanwhile, in India, the government abandoned its community development programme in 1978 (Midgely, 1986).

Over the past ten years, the idea of participation has enjoyed something of a renaissance. As Smillie (1995) pointed out, this is partly a question of the 'circle game: the painted ponies go round and round'. However, other factors were at work too. During the 1980s, as economic growth benefited some, but not others, there was increasing awareness of the plight of people who were left out, including women, disabled people, indigenous peoples and, in some cases, entire countries. In addition, as we saw from Chapter 2, the techniques of participation had improved, and there were tools available to deal with the difficulties of obtaining broad-based and equitable representation. Moreover, governments began to see the limitations of what they could achieve without engaging with civil society, and the new public management spearheaded by Aotearoa/New Zealand involved participatory approaches to governance.

The idea of participatory governance has caught on and is now in vogue among many international institutions. The World Bank, for example, considers 'participation' as a means of making its development projects function better, of helping people to cope with the economic consequences of adjustment policies and of countering the threat to governability posed by the rising exclusion of people policies. It also looks to participation as an indispensable dimension of environmental and population-control policies. The World Bank is turning increasingly to NGOs as executors of participatory initiatives in the belief that they are more flexible and better attuned to working with people than state technocrats and bureaucrats (Stiefel and Wolfe, 1994). It suggests (World Bank, 1994):

> *Accountability is at the heart of good governance and the effective voice of local people could best be increased by permitting greater freedom of associations in various non-governmental associations.*

The OECD has also pressed the importance of governance. It suggests that participation needs to take into account the different needs and claims of groups in civil and political society. The OECD has suggested that, regardless of the broader debates over donor-agency governance policies, participation, pluralism and accountability, greater effort will be made to take women's voices into account and to facilitate the participation of women in policy-making at institutional or local levels (OECD, 1993).

Literature from such international bodies tends to contain lofty sentiments that are couched in rhetorical prose. Fowler (1997) has been quick to spot the dangers of false promises, and has given clear guidelines on how organizations can put principles into practice, so that rhetoric can more closely approximate reality.

The current study reveals that there is a high demand for authentic participation among citizens. In Africa, a *Charter for Popular Participation in Development and Transformation* was created at a conference in 1990. It states:

> *We affirm that nations cannot be built without the popular support and full participation of people, nor can economic crisis be resolved and the human and economic conditions improved without the full and effective contribution, creativity and political enthusiasm of the majority of people.*

We believe strongly that popular participation, in essence, [is] the empowerment of people to effectively involve themselves in creating the structures, and in designing policies and programmes, that serve the interests of all, as well as to effectively contribute to the development process and share equitably in its benefits. Therefore, there must be an opening up of political processes to accommodate freedom of opinions, tolerate differences, accept consensus on issues, as well as ensure the effective participation of people and their organization and association (International Conference on Popular Participation in the Recovery and Development Process in Africa, 1990).

A workshop held in July 1994 in Kingston, Jamaica, under the auspices of the United Nations Development Programme (UNDP), reached similar conclusions. It noted a crisis of governance in the region. Symptoms of the crisis include apathy towards, and alienation from, existing political institutions and processes and increasing disregard for the norms and values of society by a growing number of individuals, especially the young. The workshop also reported that the capacity of the state to provide patronage and handouts had diminished. Participants located the crisis of governance in the failure of leaders and institutions to broaden and deepen democracy and participation in the regions.

VARIATIONS

While there was a striking similarity of view across the many diverse cultures and societies, there were systematic variations between different kinds of people in the study.

The main difference in views on what constituted a good society related to class. As discussed in Chapter 2, people in the study sample were classed into ordinary citizens, citizens' leaders and citizens in positions of influence.

These three groups appeared to define a good society in different ways. Most ordinary citizens were concerned with basic needs. This was most marked for ordinary citizens living in conditions of deprivation and hardship.

Citizens in positions of influence and many citizens' leaders, on the other hand, placed higher priority on issues of participation. Some ordinary citizens in better-off economic situations also stressed the importance of participation.

Association was seen as important for all groups, although it was emphasized by ordinary citizens and citizens' leaders.

Two examples, one from Malaysia and one from Belize, show how these variations worked out in practice.

Malaysia

A total of 224 people took part in the study. Nine out of ten people were individuals whose voices are rarely heard in society. They comprised young people, estate workers, factory workers, civil servants, indigenous peoples and informal-sector workers. Those interviewed were balanced to include people of different ages, races and genders, as well as city and rural dwellers. People of higher status within civil society, including community leaders, were also interviewed.

Working-class people – estate workers and informal-sector workers – were particularly concerned about basic needs and their opportunities to earn a decent livelihood. A Chinese construction worker noted:

> *I want to earn a living, save some money, buy a house that can shelter my children so that they can have a good night's sleep, provide them with a good education. But now we don't even have a house and we have to rent one. There is not enough money to send my children for a good education. It is really difficult. Now there are very few jobs for construction workers because of the economic slowdown, so our income is very irregular. It is very hard.*

While the working classes were very concerned about 'rice and cooking oil issues', the middle classes were concerned about human rights such as justice, freedom and democracy. As an academic noted:

> *When you talk about civil society, the basic concepts of freedom, democracy and politics emerged. Politics will tell you the basic issues of the society. It's fundamental liberty. If you don't have it, you'll have to promote it. It's unlikely that you would want to promote other values.*

Belize

The rich ethnic mix of Belizean society was fully represented among the 98 people who took part in the study. Women and men from all different ethnic groups were interviewed, including individuals who are normally excluded from society, such as deaf people, homeless men and gang members.

In response to the question 'what is a good society', people tended to cite fulfilment of basic needs. Most wanted jobs, access to services – particularly education, which was stressed by almost all – and a clean and safe place in which to live.

In addition, there was an emphasis on relations between people. A homeless man spoke eloquently when he said:

> *A good society is like building a house together.*

Equality was emphasized, too – particularly among those people who felt that they were discriminated against, such as people disabled by virtue of being deaf.

Among those who were better placed in society, the issue of democracy was more important. A community leader noted:

> *A good society is a democratic way of life where people participate in the decision-making process.*

The most influential people in Belizean society saw a good society in holistic terms. This involved a combination of different factors: honest politicians, stable families, sound communities, good education, political sensitivity and sound economic underpinnings. As one influential person put it:

A good society is where people have the wherewithal to establish sustainable development, access to good jobs and good health.

ASPECTS OF A GOOD SOCIETY

Notwithstanding variations of opinion, there was a large measure of agreement that a good society is one where basic needs are met, needs for association are fulfilled and opportunities for participation are encouraged. A good society depends, therefore, upon a blend of economic, social and political factors.

The way in which these three components join together suggests a hierarchy of needs that, if met, constitutes a good society. In the study, if people's basic needs were not met, they tended to see a good society in terms of the fulfilment of basic needs. If their basic needs were met, they tended to look further 'up' the hierarchy of needs. An important conclusion is that a good society is not just a matter of money. Material factors are necessary, but do not constitute a sufficient condition of a good society.

This is illustrated from the findings of two countries who took part in the study: Tuvalu and Nigeria.

Tuvalu

There was a general consensus emerging from Tuvalu that a good society was one where people are happy, peaceful and have a harmonious life. Most people added that a good life involves people working together for common goals for the benefit of society.

Behind these views was a strong sense of the importance of culture and tradition, and the importance of religion in people's lives. An older person said:

God for Tuvalu; Tuvalu for God.

There was remarkable agreement across different groups in the study on the views of a good society. Even youth, who might be expected to want different things, stressed that a good life is:

...a simple life without money.

Nigeria

There was consensus among all citizens that a good society cannot be defined solely in terms of economic indicators, but that happiness and hopefulness are more important.

Citizens of Nigeria wanted the state to combat and overcome poverty in all its social forms. At the same time, they suggested that important determinants of a good society include the extent to which all citizens are aware of their rights and responsibilities, together with their readiness to discharge their duties to society.

Citizens' leaders emphasized the importance of citizens mobilizing themselves to demand and defend their rights, and to be good followers to back up the leadership. They stressed other factors, such as the degree of compassion, love and solidarity, and the extent to which society is at peace and free of wars. They also wanted to see disabled people and other disadvantaged sectors of society taken care of and given special support. Above all, they suggested that the extent and depth to which both leaders and followers place the fear of God ahead of everything else determines a good society.

SIGNIFICANCE OF THE FINDINGS

In the minds of citizens, a good society is a balance between a number of different forces. It is one where basic needs are catered for, needs for association are met and opportunities for participation are available.

These findings about the balanced character of a good society are supported by other studies. Having reviewed the evidence, Wright (2000) suggests that there is a clear connection between a nation's per-capita GDP and the average happiness of its citizens. However, the strength of the connection comes from countries in the bottom three-quarters of the GDP scale. Once a country has a reasonably average income level, set at around US$10,000, the need for income is more or less satisfied and other factors become important for happiness. To put this another way, money and material matters are a necessary but not a sufficient condition of happiness. Argyle (1987) suggested that happiness depended on 'well-being' not on 'being well off'.

An age-old question now arises. Can we see a good society in practice? This is the topic of the following chapter.

CHAPTER 4

Friends and Enemies
of a Good Society

The society has become evil (plantation worker in Sri Lanka).

I fear that I am unable to call our present society good (female resident of Kiribati).

Achievements...are not happening at all (Creole man in Belize).

INTRODUCTION

We saw in Chapter 3 that citizens produced a coherent model of a good society based on the satisfaction of three wants: basic needs, association and participation. In this chapter, we assess the extent to which these wants were satisfied, and the extent to which good societies existed among the 47 countries.

The empirical data show that citizens based their assessments on many different factors, reaching a balanced judgement on the basis of the evidence of their perceptions. For the most part, societies fell a long way short of being good according to the criteria that individuals set out in Chapter 3. Even in countries where there had been marked economic progress, leading to increased income and greater access to modern amenities, most ordinary citizens felt that the realities of life were a long way from what was desirable. In only four countries did citizens conclude that their societies were good, and even here citizens were able to identify dark forces that threatened the continued existence of a good society.

The main emphasis in this chapter is, therefore, on the gaps between the ideal and the real, an analysis that paves the way for identifying means to fill the gaps.

WIDESPREAD DISILLUSION

Disenchantment about the state of society was widespread across the Commonwealth. In 43 out of 47 countries that took part in the study, the conditions of a good society were not met.

In the Caribbean, very few citizens could find elements of a good society. Many, particularly in Belize and Guyana, but also some in Jamaica, said that they saw no semblance of a good society.

In Asia, different voices suggested different forms of despair, disappointment and dissatisfaction, although citizens in Malaysia and Singapore were relatively more satisfied because there were greater economic opportunities, and living standards were higher.

In Africa, save for Mauritius and the Seychelles, there was widespread disaffection that took on different forms in different countries. Young people in Kenya and the Gambia cited unemployment and harassment by the police. Undefined land ownership rights surfaced as key problems in Zimbabwe, Namibia and South Africa. From all countries, women spoke about their domestic problems, poverty and their lack of power in the political process. Problems were compounded almost everywhere by the existence of massive debt burdens and the deleterious consequences of structural adjustment policies.

In the Pacific region, no country was able to achieve its citizens' vision of a good society. Across the board, Pacific citizens said that their expectations of the role of government and other actors were not being met. There was growing distrust because governments had become uncaring, elitist and divorced from their own people. While citizens neglected their responsibilities, other actors pursued the narrow aspirations of their organizations, rather than meeting the wider needs of the communities whom they were established to serve.

In the four developed countries of the Commonwealth – Aotearoa/New Zealand, Australia, Canada and the UK, there was a paradox. On the one hand, developed countries were enjoying a high and rising standard of life, there was no war and democracies were stable. On the other, there was much angst and anomie in the population, so that almost everyone who took part in the study in these countries denied the existence of a good society (Waldren, 1999).

The following five examples illustrate commonly occurring situations. The examples have been selected from different parts of the globe. Any one of the 43 countries could have provided examples. The five were chosen were selected to cover different regions, and because they typified problems that occurred elsewhere.

Kenya

'No, no way!' was the ringing denial of one respondent when asked if a good society existed in Kenya, a country straddling the Equator in East Africa. This view was widely shared among Kenyan citizens.

Chief among the factors seen as militating against a good society were: poverty and the rising price of basic commodities; declining standards of education and public services; and corruption and unresponsiveness on the part of government.

Citizens said that corruption was endemic to all levels of society, from local police forces to holders of political office. Office holders were said to be appointed on the basis of bribery or family influence and, as such, were more concerned with serving the interests of their patrons than of the community at large. The views of the poorer sections of Kenyan society went unheard so that justice, it was felt, was dispensed on the basis of wealth and influence. The charmed circle of place and office had begun to change since the introduction of the multiparty state in 1992. Although government had been slow to respond, some believed that moves towards a greater degree of democracy were now underway.

Nevertheless, in the meantime people had lost faith in the will and capacity of institutions to address the problems that Kenyan society faced, although it was notable that many of them saw effective leadership as crucial to achieving a good society.

There was a growing gulf between rich and poor. This showed up in a number of ways, most notably in access to jobs and influence. In education, lack of subsidy meant that school fees, schoolbooks and equipment had to be bought by parents, a situation that hit the poor hardest. Rising prices of basic commodities drove poor people to extra-legal activities, such as theft and prostitution.

Additional worries about Kenyan society were expressed about the security of life and property, alcohol and drug abuse, and deterioration of urban amenities.

Guyana

Situated on the north-east shoulder of South America, Guyana has one of the lowest population densities in the world. It is also, despite being comparatively rich in natural resources, the poorest country in the Commonwealth Caribbean.

Citizens generally commented on the absence of a good society. Causes for dissatisfaction were: the high cost of basic commodities; falling standards of education and public services; poor physical and social infrastructure; and an increase in crime and drug abuse.

Adverse economic conditions, particularly low wages and high rates of unemployment, made the struggle to make ends meet the number one priority. There was a prevailing sense of vulnerability and hopelessness among citizens.

Under these conditions, especially when taken in conjunction with the rigid authority of the state, there was little room for wider notions of citizenship to emerge. Even where conditions were better, individuals were seen as being relatively powerless when it came to effecting social change. This view was not confined simply to people who are normally invisible in the public domain, but was shared by citizens' leaders.

Many felt that too great a premium was placed on individual success, and the need to improve race relations was a high priority.

Pakistan

There was a tendency for ordinary citizens to describe a good society in terms of the fulfilment of basic needs. In urban areas, this usually meant the provision of health facilities, education, employment, sewerage, clean drinking water, better ecology, food, shelter, peace and security, and legally recognized equality of rights. In rural areas, people stressed the same basic necessities, though these had often an agricultural flavour: availability of fertilizers and pesticides at reasonable prices, good harvests, water for irrigation and basic roads.

Another strong theme was peace and security. All sample clusters pointed to this, and the Hindu minority was particularly concerned about it. A young Hindu said:

> Good life is unimaginable without peace and security, and in the present day situation generally in Pakistan, and particularly in Karachi, drugs and arms and ammunition are the greatest enemy of the peaceful good life for the citizens.

In some areas, particularly the North-West Frontier Province and Baluchistan, tobacco growers tended to see a good society in terms of the practice of the Qu'ran. Islam provided the solution to economic, social and political problems in the minds of these people.

Citizens' leaders and people with higher status in civil society recognized the importance of fulfilling basic needs and the conditions of peace. They also stressed more abstract ideas. Included here were religious idealism; spiritual values; tolerance in society; gender equality; freedom of speech; access to information technology; empowerment of people; cultural development; and aesthetic accomplishment.

There was a unanimous view that a good society did not exist in Pakistan. Generally, the prerequisite of peace was absent. For women security was a major problem:

> *Women are discriminated at all levels. To top it off, women are tyrannized or even raped.*

Old-style family structures inhibited women's development and made it hard for them to live a good life.

Both men and women agreed that basic necessities were not met, and that conditions of democratic government left much to be desired. There was a widespread view that government was both inefficient and corrupt:

> *There is nothing new to say about government officials. Everybody knows about their congenital habit of taking bribery.*

The government had, over successive generations, undermined the autonomy of citizens. Whenever people have voiced their desire for equal rights and social and political freedom, this has been seen as tantamount to insurrection. The government has recently waged a campaign against NGOs, particularly women's NGOs. Citizens said that such an adverse climate bred aggressive people with a negative approach to life. Many citizens felt that they had no power, no recognized role and, therefore, felt little stake in society. This had created a vacuum, which fundamentalist beliefs, sectarian hatreds and mob rule were beginning to fill.

Samoa

Samoa is a group of four islands in the South Pacific about half way between Hawaii and New Zealand.

A good society, according to the people of Samoa, should operate at two main levels. The first level was to satisfy basic needs, and the second to live peacefully and harmoniously together in families and communities. A Samoan farmer put the desire for the satisfaction of basic needs like this:

> *Samoan society can be really good if everyone works on the plantation. If every family has a plantation comprising of bananas, yams, taamu, cocoa and copra, there will be no problem [with] food.*

Culture and tradition were considered integral features of a good society in Samoa. The family-based leadership and chief structures, blended with Christianity, would bring peace and stability.

Particular groups wanted specific things from a good society. Women wanted an equitable society where their rights were acknowledged. Young people wanted empowerment. Disabled people thought that a good society existed where people did not make fun of disabled people, but took care of them instead.

Community leaders and people of high status in civil society had a more holistic view of a good society, seeing it as a combination of different features:

> *...having access to money, food, good house, good* Matai *(family leader) and good education.*

Although some people suggested that Samoa was a good society because of its traditions, most of those interviewed felt that society was changing rapidly, so that Western values and aspirations were replacing traditions and customs. The extended family, which acted as a social safety net, was disintegrating. The culture of sharing was being replaced with a culture of price. Redistribution of wealth by chiefs was now minimal, and people were becoming self-seeking and individualistic. One of the reasons that traditional community life was dying was that many found it too expensive to honour village obligations. The system involves members paying donations towards village funds, and some families found this to be onerous.

A woman suggested:

> *There is not enough money to go around to support village activities. Families moan and groan about the pressure on them to contribute towards the village expenses. We feel we have to contribute because we don't want to incur the wrath of God and endure public disgrace, but it often means that we don't have enough to feed the family.*

A young man said:

> *One is continually under pressure not only to meet obligations [to] the extended family [but to] the church and other village institutions. It is impossible to save.*

Another strand was the government. Many felt that the government did not offer value for money. Others complained of corruption. A farmer noted:

> *Sometimes you have to fork out of your pocket to get things done.*

Young people complained about the generation gap:

> *Samoan society is good, but there is a growing gap between the young and the older generation.*

Some women complained about the abuse of women and the problem of domestic violence.

Many social ills were related to economic transition. Traditionally, the economy has been dependent upon aid from abroad, private family remittances and agricultural exports. At the time of the study, the economy was undergoing major restructuring based on IMF conditions, leading to downsizing within the public sector and privatization. Some state enterprises were being sold to foreign investors.

The United Kingdom

The UK is located in Western Europe and is one of the world's great trading powers and financial centres.

Citizens in the study suggested that the central element of a good society was a sense of community. There was a variety of definitions, although most citizens stressed the importance of trust. When it existed, trust enabled people to interact with each other and with institutions. Flowing from trust were personal safety, freedom and a sense of being in control. Trust was viewed as fragile and, once lost, difficult to rebuild.

There was a gap between citizens' notions of a good society and the social and political realities of the UK. Citizens said that levels of trust in society had fallen away in recent years. Many talked of increasing trends of selfishness, cynicism and greed. As a result, notions of community had deteriorated. The mobility of the population was perceived as an influencing factor in the decline of the community. A further dimension was the increased economic insecurity caused by economic change and the introduction of the flexible labour market, which for many people meant long hours for low pay without a fixed tenure of employment.

There was a big emotional gulf between individuals and institutions. Many people felt that individual politicians were compromised once they were in positions of power and looked after themselves and their interests, rather than the interests of the collective good. Despite a growing economy and decreasing population, there was a strong sense of disquiet that prevented people from feeling good about themselves or the UK's prospects.

Summing up the sense of malaise

What comes across in these countries, as in many others, is a profound sense of malaise. In most countries, basic needs were not met, the need for association was not fulfilled and participation was absent. Even in the UK, where basic needs are generally met, there was a marked sense of alienation.

The following quotations from different parts of the world, first used in the epigraph for this chapter, sum up the mood of many citizens in the study:

> *The society has become evil* (plantation worker in Sri Lanka).

> *I fear that I am unable to call our present society good* (female resident of Kiribati).

> *Achievements...are not happening at all* (Creole man in Belize).

At the same time, it is important to acknowledge that not all citizens saw their society as irremediably bad or bereft of some elements of a good society. Rather, the feeling existed that dark forces had come to dominate.

GOOD SOCIETIES

There were four countries in which significant numbers of citizens said that they lived in a good society: Mauritius, the Seychelles, Trinidad and Tobago and Malaysia. We begin with a brief case study of each.

Mauritius

Mauritius is composed of the islands of Mauritius, Rodrigues, St Brandon and Agalega in the Indian Ocean, east of Madagascar in Southern Africa.

Citizens set out their criteria of a good society as one based on peace and harmony, economic prosperity and employment for all. Citizens' leaders said that in a good society, there would be respect, caring and honesty, a good environment, transparency and accountability, low inflation, good governance, low stress and reasonable taxation. Other values mentioned included integrity, a strong work ethic and timely adaptation to change.

Most citizens regarded Mauritius as a good society because there was economic progress, basic needs were met, crime was low and the country was safe politically. Citizens' leaders agreed and pointed to additional factors, including well-educated people and the thriving tourist industry that brought in revenue to enable the state to sustain development programmes. They stressed unity in the country and the lack of political manipulation.

The society also had a shadow. People complained about exorbitant food prices, a growing culture of materialism and a breakdown of respect for elders. People also saw growing unemployment, lack of civic education and a weakening of the family, alongside a lack of leisure facilities. Citizens feared change, particularly if it brought increased alcohol intake, drug abuse, child labour, racism, more gender inequality and restrictions on freedom of the press.

On balance, positive forces outweighed negative ones. The strength of the society appeared to rest on a good economy, a well-established system of welfare services and a sense of trust and unity among the people.

The Seychelles

The Republic of Seychelles is an archipelago of 115 islands situated in the south-western Indian Digue.

Ordinary citizens of the Seychelles believed that a good society was based on love and understanding. People should respect each other, work together without discrimination and be free to express opinions. There should be equal opportunity to enjoy education and social and economic welfare. There should be respect and harmony between the young and the old, and assistance to the elderly. The year 1998 was declared the year of caring and sharing.

Although individuals who unequivocally said that the Seychelles was a good society were in the minority, almost everyone believed that the Seychelles was on the right track. The key was racial harmony. People said that foreigners were not harassed and that everyone 'blends in'. One citizen compared the Seychelles to 'Noah's ark', commenting that 'we are all here'.

Again, there was a shadow. People complained about declining values, evidenced in the increased use of drugs and alcohol, coupled with the rising crime rate. Others pointed to rising prices, a growing culture of greed and a mentality of reliance on social welfare.

Secondary data revealed that the good society of the Seychelles was based on a stable middle-income economy, yielding enough work and money to pay for food and the essentials of life. There was an established welfare state and a culture of tolerance and respect among one of the most multiracial societies in the world.

Trinidad and Tobago

Trinidad and Tobago are tropical islands in the Caribbean, 12 kilometres north-east of Venezuela.

Citizens described a good society as safe and free from crime and poverty and where there would be respect for human life. It would have social order, common ground and equality, as well as justice and equity in the workplace and family life, so that everybody would have a stake in its existence. Importantly, too, there would be sharing and harmony between races. Society would be progressive, with clearly defined standards and norms. A good society would therefore be united and balanced in its economic, political and social dimensions.

Many ordinary citizens thought that such a good society actually existed in Trinidad and Tobago. Such a view was usually present when people had close family ties, a strong community base and were able to exercise their spirituality in practical ways.

In contrast, others stated categorically that their vision of a good society did not exist. They cited social inequalities – uneven distribution of wealth, corruption, segregation, the trampling of rights, and the absence of justice – as the major factors in the absence of a good society.

These mixed responses appeared to reflect the rapid change that had taken place in recent years. Although the economy had shown major improvement in gross domestic product, debt service payments and inflation, such benefits had not trickled down to the bulk of the population, so that the benefits did not feel 'real'. Economic restructuring meant that society had become polarized between the rich and the poor.

Older people still felt that, on the whole, they lived in a good society; but for many of these indivuals, mounting poverty, inequality and rising crime were signs of society going wrong.

Malaysia

Malaysia is located in South-East Asia. The country is divided geographically and politically into two parts. One part is a peninsula on the Asian mainland, the other forms one-third of the island of Borneo.

For Malaysians, there was much agreement that a good society should be based on racial harmony, fairness, peace, political stability, security and safety, tolerance and cooperation. As a multiracial society, it was important that people should be united, accepting and inclusive, despite their differences. A corollary was the importance of equal opportunities in jobs and education.

Although some people said that Malaysia was a good society in certain respects, they also said that the harmony upon which it depended was superficial. Beneath the surface, there was racial tension and polarization. There was also a culture of fear because of the perceived risk of state retribution. There was a general view that Malaysia had a strong state and a weak civil society. Following the collapse of the economy in 1997, stresses and strains had become more evident.

Characteristics of a good society

When comparing the responses of these four countries with the criteria of a good society, it was clear that two of the three criteria had been met: basic needs and association. The issue of participation was less clear.

In terms of basic needs, it was evident that for most people these were provided. Although none of the countries was rich, all had middle-level incomes with equitable distribution of resources, so that there was sufficient work and wealth to provide for people. In addition, in two of the countries, there was a welfare state tradition that provided a safety net.

Needs for association were also met. People felt safe and secure in their relations with other people, and there was a long history of racial harmony and a culture of tolerance. People put great emphasis on the importance of the family, community and cultural traditions.

Participation did not emerge as a particularly strong desire on the part of respondents. There appeared to be a special factor at work that made people less interested in politics than they might otherwise have been. This was the presence of a strong spiritual tradition, with the concomitant notion that God, rather than secular leadership, was the ultimate arbiter of human destiny. Such a perspective appeared to ward off materialistic desires or political ambitions of the conventional type.

We may conclude from this analysis of the four 'good societies' that not all of the three preconditions outlined at the beginning of this chapter (meeting of basic needs, association and participation) must be present. Nor did all of the respondents in these societies need to agree that a good society existed. Good societies tended to be present when a significant number of respondents in these societies thought that a balance of good over evil had been achieved, so that a deficit in one of the key areas was offset by an advantage in another.

It is important to note that all four countries had a shadow hanging over them. This shadow consisted of dark forces that threatened to tip the balance from a 'good' to a 'bad' society. Citizens expressed anxiety about such forces, feeling that growing tendencies towards racial intolerance, rising crime, increased materialism and the breakdown of traditional networks of knowledge and authority were conducive to disaffection. Citizens felt that they were in the midst of a struggle to maintain social equilibrium.

From this, it appears that the essence of a good society is not that it is without problems, but that it has the capacity to deal with its problems collectively, so that the light always outshines the dark in the long run.

ENEMIES OF A GOOD SOCIETY

Despite marked differences between the countries in the study, there were themes that recurred time and time again, such as economic difficulties, community decline, increased crime and poor governance. These themes produced a catalogue of ills and insecurities, at once physical, social and economic. The following section turns to commonly occurring factors that create a bad society.

Once again, we employ the three categories of *basic needs*, *association* and *participation* that citizens in the study themselves suggested.

BASIC NEEDS

There was a widespread failure to meet basic needs. In line with the information about poverty given in Chapter 1, the problem was most marked in Africa and South Asia, although it was present elsewhere. Failure to meet basic needs was a common complaint in the Caribbean and a growing problem in the Pacific due to the growth of the cash economy and structural readjustment programmes. Providing basic needs was less likely to be a problem in South-East Asia, where the economies of Malaysia and Singapore had raised standards, though it bubbled under the surface and found expression in the voices of some citizens. In the developed countries of Aotearoa/New Zealand, Australia, Canada and the UK, meeting basic needs was generally not a problem, though it found weaker expression through worries about jobs and the economy.

The failure to meet basic needs created profound insecurities. These insecurities took on different forms and were expressed in different ways. For a vast number of citizens, *economic insecurity* was the biggest concern. While many had livelihoods, they expressed uncertainty about assuring food, water and income for their families. Globalization of markets, products and capital caused much fear for the future. 'Donkey cannot compete with the horse', was the way a farmer in Guyana described global competition. Comments from elsewhere included:

> *Being a farmer here means starving. Jobs give money and money is the way to everything here* (an elderly woman in Lesotho).

> *We are very hungry, our children are not getting enough food to grow up properly. We get poor yields from our fields because we do not have enough money to buy fertilizers* (a farmer in Swaziland).

The state of our poverty is such that we are compelled to send our little children to do labour in other cities (a rural woman in Pakistan).

Economic insecurity, as already noted, was most marked in Sub-Saharan Africa and South Asia. For instance, Lesotho, a country of slightly more that two million people totally surrounded by the Republic of Southern Africa, illustrates how economic insecurity can attack the basic fabric of society. Citizens conceived of a good society in Lesotho as a balance between 'hardware' and 'software'. The hardware consists of the materialistic underpinnings, while the software includes the values, norms and belief systems of people and their communities. In Lesotho, citizens said that the failure of the hardware was undermining the software. Values of peace, mutual help, cooperation and respect were being undermined by poverty. Citizens lamented that high levels of unemployment were fuelling ideas of theft, jealousy, hatred, revenge and witchcraft. A group of young men interviewed admitted that they were driven to thieving and selling drugs because there was no legitimate alternative.

Similar results were obtained in Malawi. Here, citizens said that they were severely debilitated by their daily struggles for survival, caused by high unemployment and inflation in basic foodstuffs. They explained that loans were not available for poor people; young people were dying of AIDS; health facilities had deteriorated; and farmers had no access to the materials they need in order to grow their crops. People said that there had been a marked increase in armed robberies, rape and tribal aggression. Disorder had spread among the political class, and politicians sometimes fought physically in public.

In many countries, the need to make a living under near impossible conditions dominated the lives and efforts of most citizens. It was a constant refrain among such peoples that this overwhelming need prevented them from discharging or even considering the higher demands of citizenship. There was a clear inverse correlation between the struggle to fulfil basic needs and the possibilities of association with others and participation in politics.

Economic insecurity was not restricted to poor countries. In the developed countries of the Commonwealth – Aotearoa/New Zealand, Australia, Canada and the UK – economies were strong, with per-capita GDP ranging from US$17,700 to US$21,400. All four countries had recently reformed their economies, intending to create a robust model capable of competing in the global marketplace. The UK had made a 20-year transition from a manufacturing economy to one based on service industries, such as insurance and banking. Canada and Aotearoa/New Zealand had made the transition from an agrarian-based economy to one both more industrialized and urbanized. Australia had increased its export of manufactured goods, building on its comparative advantage in minerals, metals and fossil fuels. In the past 50 years, the gross product of the developed countries of the Commonwealth had increased tenfold, with growth predicted to continue because of productivity gains brought by new technology.

In all four countries, the signs and symbols of modernity were apparent everywhere – rapid consumer take-up of the latest technology, mobile phones and the internet. However, economic growth appeared to have had little effect on happiness. Indeed, such growth appeared to walk hand-in-hand with deepening afflictions and woes – drug addiction, youth suicides and broken families. Part of the problem was that the process of economic reform had produced enormous social distress. Economic transitions had produced shakeouts of labour, with whole areas losing their economic rationale. Dislocation was made worse by the global depression of the early 1990s and the Asian crisis of 1997. Consequences included greater polarity between the rich and poor, a new class of people likely to remain unemployed for the rest of their working lives and a profound sense of loss among the victims of change.

In many parts of the world, economic and institutional restructuring was a common cause of distress. It mattered little whether such restructuring was undertaken voluntarily, as in the case of the developed countries, or involuntarily because of the need to gain the support of international finance agencies, such as the IMF or the World Bank.

At present there is a deficiency... A failure in the management of the economy, such as rise of costs and inflation, interest rates, unemployment (a government minister in Zimbabwe).

The government has cut the public service; that's why there is no work (a teenage girl in the Cook Islands).

The effects of structural adjustment programmes commonly led to job insecurity in government and in industry. In many cases, such programmes were judged by citizens to be widening the gap between the rich and the poor.

Let us take the example of how structural adjustment programmes were affecting Nauru, an island in the South Pacific Ocean, 42 kilometres south of the Equator. At the time of the study, Nauru had one of the highest per-capita incomes in the developing world. This income was dependent upon the mining of phosphates, but supplies were running out fast. The government had foreseen this and had invested in trust funds to soften the blow, but had borrowed from these funds to make good a fiscal deficit. A reform programme, in association with the Asian Development Bank, was put in place in 1998. People in the study sample appeared to be in a state of shock. They faced plummeting incomes and a sense of being out of control. They had lost faith in the government because of its perceived misuse of the trust funds. One person said: 'The government have not only milked the cow; they have pulled off the udder.' There was a sense that structural reforms were creating a two-class society. One influential person commented on the 'selfishness, arrogance and the corruption in high levels of the community'.

Inequality – and, in particular, the growing polarization between 'haves' and 'have nots' – appeared to be a frequent by-product of structural adjustment programmes. We saw earlier how the 'good society' of Trinidad and Tobago was threatened by such polarization due to economic reforms.

Inequality, whatever its cause, was almost always perceived as an enemy of a good society. A comment from a fisherwoman in India was typical of many:

> *How come some people get bigger houses and cars every year while I am struggling to feed my family?*

As well as economic insecurity, citizens also felt a sense of *social insecurity* because their basic needs for services were not met. The delivery of basic services could no longer be taken for granted. People said that the quality and regularity of public services in water, transport, sanitation, electricity, education and health had declined, even in developed countries. Again, public services were often casualties of structural adjustment programmes in several countries of the Pacific, Caribbean and Africa. When privately supplied through the market, basic social services were not affordable by a majority of citizens. The consequences were that children did not go to school; mothers did not receive medicine; and older people had no care or shelter. Even where institutional safety nets existed, they often had holes that allowed vulnerable people to fall through. Many citizens, such as a rural woman in Bangladesh, a self-employed man in Uganda and an unemployed single mother in Aotearoa/New Zealand complained about going further into debt in order to take care of illness in their families:

> *...good hospitals are in urban areas and one has to walk or travel long distances. The major concern is the maternity wards that are in appalling conditions in government*

hospitals. After delivery, mother and baby sleep on the floor or under the bed of an expectant mother (a Ugandan citizen).

...there is no protection among the San people when it comes to AIDS...people do not have education (a Namibian citizen).

Jamaica was a good example of a country whose social infrastructure was damaged by conditions attached to IMF loans. Cuts in public expenditure led to reductions in education and health provision, as well as lower living standards caused by job losses in domestic industries when markets were opened up to international competition. Many citizens attributed the woes of the country to these forces, suggesting that lack of jobs, low educational opportunities and poverty had fed the crime rate.

Compounding social insecurity was a growing sense of *physical* insecurity. War and terrorism were present in many parts of the Commonwealth. In all war zones, citizens said that war had destroyed all semblance of a good society. In Sri Lanka, people emphasized that a good society could not coexist with conflict:

A good society does not exist in this country. This is evident when observing the loss of lives (and limbs) in the north-east war...and broken up families and people who have lost their homes...there should be reconciliation to promote a country that is not governed by weapons... It is essential to have peace and unity. Expenditure on war could be used on youth issues (unemployment, education, industry, etc). The state can contribute by ending the war and bringing about peace...through discussion and negotiation.

No matter what the location, the costs of the war appeared huge, both in material and in human terms. In the Karachi area of Pakistan and the Chittagong hill areas of Bangladesh, persistent war has consumed thousands of lives, entailed huge military budgets and sapped the morale of people affected. Sierra Leone was already the world's poorest country before the war made the situation far worse. Citizens in that war-torn country lamented the widespread hatred, greed, avarice, dishonesty and disrespect for public property. Citizens complained of human rights abuses, summary executions and harassment of defenceless citizens. At the same time, the government's inability to end the rebel war had awakened citizens' groups, so that there was now a groundswell of opinion at grassroots level in favour of a return to multiparty democracy.

In addition to the acute problem of war, citizens complained about the chronic societal problems of drugs and alcohol abuse. Such problems made some neighbourhoods in many countries unsafe. People related stories of crime, assault, robbery and murder. Citizens often said that they felt unsafe at home and on the streets. They worried for their children's security, and in many countries women felt insecure at home and outdoors:

Women and children are not safe, as rapists are released through bribe (a citizen leader in Malawi).

ASSOCIATION

Association was under attack. Traditional bonds of family and kinship were threatened by the pressures of work, urbanization and migration. The growth of a consumer culture and the desire for material well-being was pushing citizens to become self-centered and individualistic. Moral values based on materialism were replacing those based on contentment, spirituality, mutual help and generosity:

Singaporean society emphasizes five 'Cs' – car, cash, credit card, condominium and career. Singaporeans aspire to one wife, two children, three rooms, four wheels and a five-figure salary (young professional in Singapore).

Across all continents processes of association were being disturbed by the winds of economic change. Citizens were being driven by new economic imperatives and were losing touch with the customs, duties and obligations to other people that had once formed the bedrock of their lives. They felt out of control and could not understand what was happening.

The example of Papua New Guinea illustrates this trend. A total of 45 people were consulted in the study. About two-thirds of these were ordinary citizens, and the remainder were community leaders or people of higher status within civil society. People interviewed included women, young people, farmers and growers, government officials, social agencies and executives from the coffee industry.

There was general agreement that a good society is life in a traditional village community, where people meet obligations and responsibilities to one another, and abide by the social order of the village community. A community activist put it like this:

> *Everyone in the society must appreciate they are one unit with various potentials, energies, gifts, knowledge, experiences to do something to help themselves.*

For women, the good society involved men recognizing their responsibility in the relationship between men and women. The well-being of children is inseparable from the well-being of the women who bear and nurture them. A woman leader said:

> *A good society is one which recognizes the role of women as mothers and wherein women have equal rights and opportunity to hold jobs and responsibility with the men. Women's health, women's education and women's participation in development will determine the health of future families and communities.*

For many people, a good society was a thing of the past. The culture was falling apart, aided by the forces of national unification and modernization. Individualism was a threat, creating development that undermined culture and bred social discord and a high crime rate. A youth leader said:

> Today, all these good features of a good society [are] fast disappearing in some places, while some are mourning over it, for it [good society] become history.

To take another example, Botswana is an economic success in comparison with its neighbours. In the study, citizens said that a good society was one in which everyone has access to education, shelter and employment, irrespective of gender, educational status, economic power or association with certain groups. They explained that in a good society, health services are accessible and affordable. Moreover, there is no war, and people believe in love, peace and negotiations. Above all, there is respect for humanity.

Most citizens said that they did not live in a good society because relationships between people had broken down. There was a tendency to look down upon disadvantaged people, such as the disabled, commercial sex workers, unemployed youths, the poor, the aged and street children. There was also a widespread concern about lawlessness. Unemployed young people were said to be roaming the streets and resorting to crime. A citizens' leader was shocked that:

> ...the boys of today rape women and children at night, in the streets, and they fight each other in the streets. The police seem to be losing the battle and the situation is becoming worse each and every day. When I came to Gaborone city in 1976, we used to walk all over this city at night. Today, walk in the street at night and tomorrow you are dead.

In the developed countries of the Commonwealth, processes of association also appeared to be under considerable strain. In Australia, citizens identified a mix of factors, including rapid and dramatic social and economic change, changes in social values and life styles and the difficulty society experienced in sustaining some of its traditional forms in the modern world.

While economic change was opening up remarkable new opportunities for sustainable prosperity, it was also visiting on whole communities the wrenching dislocation of massive structural change that can sap confidence and cohesion. In addition, there was a rapid growth in the complexity by which people define the boundaries of their lives' responsibilities (Sturgess, 1996). Traditionally, association tended to occur in the places in which people lived: their physical communities. Now, people are as likely to be connected and loyal to communities of interest and commitment whose reach is global or national, as well as local.

The evidence from other industrialized nations suggests that processes of association are similarly under pressure. In its final report, for example, the National Commission on Civic Renewal in the United States (Pew Charitable Trusts, 1998) observed:

> *A generation ago, we realized that the degradation of our physical environment was the result of countless millions of decisions, by individual citizens as well as large corporations, and that if we really wanted to clean it up we would have to change our habits as well as our laws. The degradation of our civic environment stems from similar causes and requires similar remedies. It is legitimate and honorable for a free people to work as hard to protect its moral ecology as its natural environment. As citizens, we must ask more of ourselves.*

However, many citizens in the study were withdrawing into their own skins. The past was a safe haven compared with the present, and it was easier to retreat into the glory and certainty of history and tradition. Citizens were, alternatively or additionally, exploring other ways of defining themselves. Kinship, caste, tribe, religion, sect and ethnicity were becoming powerful devices for carving out identities:

> *I do not want to be an old bag hanging on to tradition, but am afraid at the same time of my children living in the modern world* (a *Matai* – traditional chief – in Samoa).

PARTICIPATION

The need for participation was almost never met. As we saw in Chapter 3, independence from colonial rule heralded a period of new hope for citizens in the Commonwealth. Many post-colonial plans had ordinary people playing big parts in the development of society – through community development in agriculture, social services and education. But the early promises of leaders and officials were not fulfilled, and people soon felt that development schemes and other government initiatives failed to benefit the vast majority. The findings of the current study reveal a growing disillusionment of citizens with their governments.

The case of India illustrates a commonly occurring problem for government. In the quarter century following independence in 1947, development in India was characterized by centralized economic planning and a form of democracy inherited from the UK. This 'Nehruvian model' was challenged by growing social movements because it was seen as elitist and failed to deliver benefits to the mass of Indian people. However, by the time reform came in the 1970s, ordinary people had disengaged from the political process, regarding the system as corrupt and inefficient. The state was seen as having two oppressive pillars: dominance and incompetence. As an example of this, the police were frequently described as enemies, as opposed to protectors, of the people.

Citizens in many parts of the Commonwealth suggested that government policies and programmes did not benefit vast sections of the people. Based on evidence from secondary data, their views were accurate. For example, after 50 years, the record of the state-led model of development in South Asia is dismal. Two-thirds of the people are poor, accounting for nearly half of the world's poor; and more than 60 per cent of the people are illiterate, accounting for two-thirds of the world's illiterate people. Economic security is a major issue because people in these countries are facing a daily struggle for survival. Those in the subsistence economy are hungry and malnourished; those in the modern economy are vulnerable and underpaid. The cost of living increases, and low rates of economic growth and a skewed distribution of access and assets have combined to accentuate the sense of economic insecurity among vast sections of the population. The economic liberalization and private-sector development model reached these countries only at the beginning of the 1990s (although Sri Lanka began to liberalize in the late 1970s). This has resulted in further changes in labour-market and employment patterns, thereby increasing insecurity for those who previously had secure public-sector employment for life (SAARC, 1992).

Similar findings were obtained in Africa. According to a 1997 briefing paper entitled 'Revitalizing the OAU', authored by a former Organization for African Unity (OAU) employee:

> *33 years on, now, Africa is pervaded by a sense of disappointment. Several of its countries are beset by instability, civil war and ethnic carnage. Economically, Africa has performed poorly – with the exception of a few countries, producing less food per capita than...at independence. A sizeable part of its population now lives on handouts from a compassionate international community. And its early modest achievement in expanding school enrolment and primary health care now appears unsustainable. The future seems even bleaker. Population pressures, environmental degradation and the scourge of*

AIDS have set loose disastrous social and economic consequences. Africa is losing ground in international trade, in technology and in other areas of competitiveness, not only to the industrialized world, but also to a growing number of Third World countries, earning for several of its countries such accolades as 'the poorest of the poor' and 'the Third World's Third World' (cited in Chigudu, 2000).

African people have felt frustrated by failed programmes, and attribute such failure to the fact that policies and programmes have not been grounded in people's own perceptions of the problems, priorities and solutions. The imposed priorities and solutions can be sustained only through external support and collapse as soon as the support is terminated.

The perceived widespread failure of government had led citizens to a confidence crisis in their governments. Such a gap between governments and their people was a near universal finding in the study and is widely supported by evidence from other studies (Norris, 1999; Knight and Stokes, 1996; Putnam, 2000).

It was noticeable that, in many of the states where respondents felt that a good society did not exist, there was a tradition of strong central authority. Moreover, it was precisely in these countries where people were inclined to look to the state as the main agent in bringing about decisive social change. Such findings from the study reflect a profound ambiguity. On the one hand, accustomed as they were to thinking of the state as the source of all effective authority, citizens were unable to conceive of any other means of radical change. On the other hand, they were aware that the state was failing them, and that its virtually exclusive possession of power meant that their autonomy and their ability to check the abuses of state power – and to lobby it for what they wanted – were seriously impaired.

There was, therefore, something of a dependency syndrome. To explain this, we have to look back to the time when governments became independent. Rather than emerging from the social structures of their countries, many Commonwealth governments were implants from outside. The new systems of legislature, executive and judiciary gradually strengthened their hold on these countries. Extensive government bureaucracies, electoral politics and common-law jurisprudence became the infrastructure of nation states. Strong bureaucracy and powerful law-and-order machinery spread government control throughout the length and breadth of these countries.

As the centralized state apparatus began to control natural resources, public policies and political decision-making, it acquired hegemony over the lives, and slowly the minds, of ordinary people. Through its interventionist and provider roles, sometimes in the name of socialism and sometimes acting for the cause of the welfare state, the ruling political elite developed a paternalistic approach towards its people.

This pattern was true of most South Asian countries, except Malaysia. For example, Pakistan:

> *...had suffered at the hands of elitist bureaucrats, arrogant generals, opportunist feudalists, bigoted* mullahs *and a regionalized intermediate class. Both the state and the civil society needed a new relationship rooted in the humanness of the society and supremacy of political culture* (Malik, 1997).

In other areas of the Commonwealth, this pattern of government could also be found. In the Caribbean, it was noted: 'Belize today suffers from economic distress, social decay and ministerial abuse of power and bureaucratic inertia' (Spear, 1997). The Belizean state was said to exercise virtually absolute control over social and economic life, from the provision of social services to the marketing of primary products. Similarly, in Africa, where the legacy of colonialism had removed tribal geography and destroyed the moral order upon which people depended for stability, governments had little prospect of forging a sense of national purpose, public good or social welfare. Typically, African governments have involved an overblown public sector, protecting public industries without addressing the structural problems of the agrarian economies that affect the mass of the population and require strategic intervention in land reform, credit availability and selective subsidy to ensure that agriculture can perform well. In the Pacific Islands, citizens perceived that governments had become uncaring, elitist and divorced from their own people.

The distancing of government concerns from the lives of ordinary people weakened customary forms of accountability and, on occasion, led to a highly corrupt, self-seeking, inefficient and partisan state. In these cases, political parties and leaders, government officials and other vested interests connived to divert enormous public resources for narrow and selfish private benefit and use. The policies, laws and procedures of the state began to be selectively implemented and applied. Public servants and elected political leaders became 'more equal than others'. The politics of vote banks was used to reinforce existing divisions within society and to create new ones by pampering one community and ignoring others. These already stratified and diverse societies became even more fragmented and conflict ridden. Even in Malaysia, the public service has become too loyal to the ruling political party and shows signs of ethnic divide (Puthucheary, 1998).

Corruption and self-seeking behaviour among political leaders and public officials were highly damaging to the trust that citizens had in their governments. The study revealed high levels of suspicion among citizens about the motives and intentions of their governments. They felt ignored or even betrayed by their elected representatives. By association, they became suspicious of the very programmes and agencies that were created to meet their needs. The result was a wholesale collapse of people's faith in institutions:

The leaders have big salaries and people are without food
(a citizen in Zimbabwe).

The result was a sense of powerlessness:

We are not in a position to complain to anyone as there is
nobody who listens to us – not even the police (a citizen in
Gambia).

Poor people like us have no role to play... No one ever
listens to us (a free-trade zone worker in Sri Lanka).

Local government where we vote for councillors has done
nothing for us. Their role was supposed to focus on local
affairs and difficulties, but nothing is done to that effect
(urban resident in South Africa).

Many citizens felt afraid to speak up because, whether openly or
quietly, many democratic governments repressed dissent and
disagreements. Political leaders and public officials, in the
experience of citizens, did not like to hear criticism, blame or 'bad
news' – they wanted only praise, flattery and 'good news':

In small communities like ours, you pay the price of
speaking out (an influential citizen in Dominica).

We dare not voice our views because of fear (a construction
worker in Malaysia).

Respondents in Tonga, an archipelago in the South Pacific Ocean,
illustrated the fear that people felt and explained how it paralysed
progress. As chief of state of Tonga, the king appoints the prime
minister and deputy prime minister for life. The key executive body
is the privy council, composed of the king and cabinet ministers.
There is a unicameral legislative assembly with 30 seats, though

only 12 of these are elected by popular vote, with the remainder reserved for cabinet members or nobles. The citizens of Tonga expressed a sense of powerlessness. People said that they could not change things through democratic means and felt marginalized in the political process. Women felt particularly oppressed since they had no rights to own land and could play no part in decision-making. Even the government had begun to recognize that this system needed to be modernized. The deputy prime minister said: 'Tonga must rethink and reshape its institutions and ideas to retain what is best of Tonga while allowing the development of a system that meets changing aspirations and rising needs.'

Reform did not always do the trick. Aotearoa/New Zealand is often cited as the test bed for the 'new public management'. Since 1984, successive governments – first Labour and then National – have revolutionized the structure, management and role of the public sector. A remarkable coalition of politicians, businessmen and economists has forced through a contract model of government based upon a strict purchaser–provider split. Despite all of its efforts, citizens perceived the government as having an interest in 'keeping people powerless'. People said that the government failed to encourage people to participate and discriminated unfairly against indigenous peoples in its policies and practices.

There was a clear difference, however, between states that were trying to listen to citizens and those that did not. Canada, for example, had chalked up some successes in this respect. Decision-makers were aware of the growing disconnection between government and citizens and were trying to do something about it. For example, the Canadian National Forum on Health held 71 discussion groups in 34 communities across the country, reflecting diversity in demographics, ethnicity, size and economic activity, in order to ask Canadians how to improve health services. In another example, after three decades of what were, at times, glacially paced negotiations, Canada's map was redrawn and *Nunavut*, meaning 'our land' in Inuktitut, was born. The government showed that it could, eventually, listen to aboriginal groups.

Some other states were self-consciously repressive. We have already mentioned Pakistan and its crackdown on dissidents. Other regions, though perhaps less extreme, were repressive too. In Uganda, for example, the legacy of Idi Amin's psychodrama of abusive power lingered following his removal in 1979. Following disputed elections in 1981, bringing Obote to power for a second term, there was armed insurrection leading to civil war. A military junta took over in 1985, only to be overthrown by the National Resistance Movement in 1986. Although there have been significant improvements since then, the state was accused by its citizens of fanning corruption and protecting its functionaries, who divert scarce resources to personal use. People asserted that the one-party system has violated people's rights of association. Citizens emphasized that today's Uganda was characterized by immorality, corruption, nepotism, tribalism and religious sectarianism.

Needless to say, the existence of a strong top-down state, with repressive tendencies, tended to inhibit civil society. A government which arrogates the greater part of power to itself tends to be hostile to civil society organizations, whose activities are perceived as an encroachment on its own sphere of influence.

Strongly centralist states were by no means always crudely repressive. More often, they were seen simply as self-serving or favouring certain sections of the population at the expense of others. The effect on individuals' initiatives and on civil society was equally discouraging in either case. At best, a culture of dependency was created; at worst, there was a climate of fear as respondents spoke of reprisals for any criticism of the state.

In these cases, we can see a relationship between the three preconditions of a good society. In this case, the absence of *participation* militated against the fulfilment of basic needs. Governments were unable to act as providers of social and economic benefits according to the social democratic models of the mid 19th to mid 20th centuries. They were unwilling, however, to widen the charmed circle of political decision-making so that other agencies or combinations of agencies might supply their shortcomings, and they discouraged individual citizens from taking a greater responsibility in solving their own problems:

The government controls Maori today, managing us to be fractious, not to be united (a Maori youth in New Zealand).

...implementation depends on leaders and officials; those projects are implemented where they get allowances (a disabled man in Uganda).

WOMEN

So far, we have seen that citizens' assessments of their present reality are gloomy. However, some groups were affected more than others. For the women of the Commonwealth, there were significant issues. Women lamented that their interests, needs, perspectives and demands have not been represented or regarded as important. In some countries, such as Swaziland and Lesotho, women are still treated as minors.

The *United Nations Universal Declaration of Human Rights* of 1948 recognized women's rights as an integral part of human rights overall. However, in all of the Commonwealth countries, women pointed out that they do not enjoy equal rights. Even though equality before the law may have been enshrined in many legal codes, *de facto* inequality persists because of lack of enforcement. This is made worse by the fact that many women are unaware of their rights and the possibility of obtaining relief.

A Zimbabwe feminist said:

Just being a woman is in itself life threatening in many situations. In our society, women's lives are threatened by abortion and infanticide, lack of education, health care and violence against them. These threats are seen to rise in the private sphere over which the state is seen not to have any jurisdiction. Public policy in many countries is unresponsive to this threat in life.

In the opinion of citizens' leaders and citizens with high status, the absence of a true democratic culture, together with inadequate representation of women in the political process, coupled with unfair electoral laws, were indicators of the absence of a good society. They explained that the law continued to be a major culprit when it came to the structural obstacles to women's well-being. The absence of specific legal provision to deal with gender-specific forms of violence at home and in war zones was said to be particularly serious. A respondent from Bangladesh complained:

Where the law exists, there are no enforcement mechanisms clearly spelling out criminal penalties.

A Kenyan respondent pointed out that:

While law, in general, is hard to reform, customary law is even harder. In some African countries a man is allowed to have sex with his sister-in-law if the wife is barren. Given the prevalence of HIV/AIDS pandemic, the implications of this male privilege for women are obvious.

Women felt that policy-makers were unaware of the dominance of men because it was so ingrained in the values and beliefs of society. In Ghana, a higher-status citizen noted:

Economic strategies for national development are not generally deliberately designed to be biased in favour of men, but their lack of explicit consideration of gender relations means that, in practice, this often is the case.

Patriarchy produced a culture where violence against women was nothing extraordinary. Consider the following emotionally charged headlines from a Ugandan newspaper. They give a reasonable sample of what women go through on a day-to-day basis.[1]

Under rape: 'some women deserve rape', 'women woo men to rape them', 'campus girl fakes rape' and 'Matembe renews call to have rapists castrated'.

Under defilement: '74-year-old charged for defiling a kid', 'judges want defiling age at 16', 'parent forces 12-year-old pupil into marriage', 'defiled girl delivers in class', 'defiling teacher blasted', 'man, 34, defiles mentally deranged child', '"parents faking defiling", says police'.

Under domestic violence: 'violence to women worse than war', 'Kumi woman bitten to death by husband over a squirrel', 'women judges decry violence', 'Masaka man beats wife over sex', 'man bites, swallows wife's ear', 'man nails wife to death'.

Headlines in which the words 'rape', 'defile' and 'violence' feature so frequently would suggest the antithesis of a good society.

In all the countries of the Commonwealth, violence against women was acknowledged to be a global phenomenon and was painted in red as an evil that must be stamped out. Violence against women not only affected the poor, or women in the developing world, it cut across national boundaries, ideologies, class, race and ethnic groups. The UN began to recognize the problem of violence against women in the context of the UN Decade for Women, a recognition given impetus by the four major conferences on women: in Mexico City (1975), Copenhagen (1980), Nairobi (1985) and Beijing (1995). Working to raise the issues of violence against women demands special attention in view of the constraints such violence places on women's full potential.

Synthesizing the views of women in the Commonwealth, it was clear that women would never be able to enjoy a good life as long as violence in the home, in institutions, in the workplace and in war zones continued. For most women, peace was not just the absence of war (Drage, 1994).

In addition to violence, there was a range of issues that involved the oppression of women. One was the use of child labour, a phenomenon that poverty has encouraged. A miner in Tanzania observed:

Child labour is rampant. Instead of going to school, children are working in mines.

Similarly, in Lesotho, many children complained of being tired of looking after animals and going hungry.

Unemployment was a big issue. An elderly woman from Lesotho said that 'a job gives money and is the key to everything here'. A South African woman also observed: 'We cannot have good things if we are not employed.'

The majority of women in Commonwealth countries are farmers. However, they indicated that they were concerned about a lack of markets for their produce. 'Being a farmer here means starving,' mourned a South African woman. Another farmer observed:

...being a farmer, making a living off the land by dry-land cropping, gardening and livestock farming, is almost impossible, especially in Lesotho Mountains. A rapidly growing population paired with environmental decline, leading to the loss of farm and rangelands, has resulted in a decreased agricultural output in relation to the number of mouths to feed.

Education was seen as a means of economic advancement. A woman explained the importance of education:

If we were educated, we would be able to find a way of using our own wool by manufacturing blankets and other saleable items. Now we are forced to sell wool and buy goods made from our wool at very high prices.

Women complained about a lack of information, particularly about reproductive health. Women in the South said that they were not living in good societies because their community participation was perceived as being outside of the planning and development process.

Teenagers did not believe that they were living in a good society either. A 14-year-old girl believed that, while she had not experienced a good life, if the present situation persisted, it was unlikely she would experience a good life in her lifetime. Female housemaids who were all teenagers lamented that their monthly pay was extremely low, considering that they worked 12 hours daily. They complained:

We are not considered important in the eyes of our employers and the authorities; we are being segregated from the rest of society.

In Sri Lanka more than 70 per cent of rural women felt that a good society did not exist. They emphasized that there was no freedom for women in society. The women pointed out that they were afraid for their children, especially in the face of possible abuse when left alone at home.

Disabled women bemoaned their fate. They complained that the disabled did not have qualified and trained teachers. They said that the disabled were discriminated against in terms of employment, yet 'we are able'. They claimed that the lame, in particular, were discriminated against, especially pregnant women. 'Nurses are always asking us to tell them who impregnated us,' they remarked.

Most women felt that there was an increase in armed conflict, corruption, rape, tribal conflict, unemployment and the prices of commodities. They observed that loans were not available to the poor, health facilities had deteriorated, young people were dying of AIDS and farmers had no access to agricultural inputs.

What emerged from the study was that women want to see their interests put into the mainstream agenda of international development institutions, national governments, and political and civil society institutions. This would entail more than just integrating gender issues within existing development paradigms. Women said that the paradigms needed to be transformed in order to redistribute labour and resources in an equitable manner. A key step towards achieving this is to create the conditions for women to participate in determining development priorities.

Despite the inferior status accorded to women, they nevertheless appeared strong in the face of adversity. Women saw themselves as existing *outside* of the mainstream of society through oppression or discrimination. They wanted to be inside – not to be subsumed in the mainstream, but to have influence on its values and norms. They wanted equality of opportunity to enable them to become full citizens. The agenda for women was to *gain* something, and they were determined to do something to improve their situation. They had identified the main enemy as persistent gender inequality, embedded in the practices of most institutions that brokered power in society.

In many parts of the world, women were acting strategically to improve their condition. In Africa, for example, several tertiary-level institutions have been set up to pursue gender studies. In some instances, notably Uganda and South Africa, affirmative action measures have been taken to increase the representation of women in national institutions, such as the country's parliament. In Uganda, up to a third of the total membership of the national assembly is now made up of women – a direct result of such measures. Similarly, using affirmative action principles, South Africa has achieved a sizeable representation of women in key organizations. In the Caribbean, an active women's movement has made Trinidad and Tobago the first country in the region to recognize the existence of rape in marriage. There were other examples of such positive developments. Although women still felt oppressed about their situation, many felt upbeat about their prospects.

OTHER GROUPS

For men, the situation was different. Men tended to see themselves as existing inside of the mainstream of society and wanted to remain so. They feared, however, that they would lose their place because of economic changes that made their livelihoods redundant. The agenda for men was about maintaining the status quo and avoiding loss. This attitude produced widespread fear and uncertainty about the future. There was a widespread reported crisis in masculinity in which men needed to redefine themselves in the light of their changed status in relation to work and to family. Many men appeared as if they were floundering, and some appeared deeply unhappy, without having the wherewithal to do much about it. In many countries, there were steep rises in rates of alcoholism, suicide and other measures of pathology. A high prevalence of unstable men appeared to carry major risks for those who wanted a good society.

Young people appeared to be in a double bind. In common with women, young people tended to see themselves as *outside* of the mainstream of society; but unlike women they were *unsure whether they wanted to be in or out*. As a result, young people were torn between flight (alcohol, drugs, drop out) and fight (violent action, protest, conflict).

When identifying elements of a good society, young people tended to highlight the provision of basic needs (food, water and shelter) as important, ensuring the welfare of all citizens, as well as access to education for all. They spoke of societies where there was close cooperation, where poverty was displaced by educational and economic opportunity, and where there was active participation of young people in decision-making about public life. A good society would generate caring, sharing, respect, self-help, peace, respect for young people, equal treatment of citizens and racial harmony. In good societies, there would be no violence, crime or poverty, and governments would govern with the cooperation of the people, rather than against their wishes.

Sadly, few young people could find substantial elements of such a good society in their countries. Young people raised concerns about poverty, war, famine, family breakdown, rising crime, violence, rape, drug and alcohol abuse, and the growing threat of HIV/AIDS. In response, many young people had opted out, leading to civic leaders in some countries talking about 'the lost generation'. Young people felt confused and let down by the world that their elders had created.

CHAPTER 5

Good Governance

Vikings of the new sunrise...we must be hopeful! (a Maori poem).

INTRODUCTION

In Chapter 3, we looked at citizens' views of their ideal society and, in Chapter 4, at what they said was real. We have concluded that the gap between the ideal and the real is enormous. In this respect, the study has reached its lowest ebb. To turn this around, we now move on to the practical – that is, citizens' views of how to bridge the gap between the ideal and the real.

We look at what citizens say that governments should be doing, at what they say citizens should be doing themselves and at what other organizations should be doing to bring about an improved society. Together, these actions add up to governance, defined earlier in this book as 'collective decision-taking and action in which government is one stakeholder among others'. The purpose of this chapter is to find the combination of actions that makes up good governance, defined as 'collective decision-taking and action that leads to the common public good'.

DIFFERING CHALLENGES

In Chapter 4, it was clear that there was a diversity of challenges, varying according to political context, level of social and economic development and the speed of change. There were five main kinds of challenges.

The first challenge was to retain aspects of a good society where it already existed. In Mauritius, the Seychelles, Malaysia and Trinidad and Tobago, it was important to conserve those characteristics that produced a good society and to resist the incursion of those that threatened it.

The second challenge was to renew existing practices in older democracies. This applied particularly to Australia, Canada, Aotearoa/New Zealand and the UK, although the need for such renewal was also present in some developing countries. Governments had, in some cases, already begun to reform themselves in response to increased economic expectations and growing demands from citizens. However, it was clear that all countries had some way to go in inspiring their citizens to support public institutions.

The third challenge was to deal with the exigencies of a globalized culture. This affected many island nations of the Pacific, some Caribbean communities and some African countries. With greater exposure to world influences, notably through travel and telecommunications, these countries faced an erosion of their traditional mores and a threat to their moral order. The main issue was how to achieve a balance between the conflicting forces of continuity and change.

A fourth challenge was how to face up to extreme adversarial situations and circumstances. War, dictatorship and internal violence were present in Sri Lanka, Sierra Leone, Pakistan and India, among other countries. These conditions carried high risk and were inimical to notions of a good society.

A final challenge was the lack of direction in policies and practices. Many countries of the Commonwealth lacked clear ideas about how to respond to internal and external pressures, and appeared to be muddling along. As a result, there was a sense of confusion in the relationship between state and citizens, characterized by uneasy blends of conflict and cooperation, repression and responsiveness, as well as apathy and support.

Notwithstanding these enormous challenges, we saw in Chapter 3 that citizens were, by and large, optimists. In Chapter 4, we saw that they were also realists because their optimism was heavily tempered by the reality of their situation. In this chapter we will see that, despite a degree of skepticism and cynicism, citizens were far from indifferent about the future of their societies. While expressing a sense of powerlessness in acting alone, observing that unsupported individual efforts can make little difference in the face of the intractable forces of current reality, many said that they were hopeful. They fulfilled the Maori dream that formed the epigraph of this chapter: 'Vikings of the new sunrise...we must be hopeful!'

STATE ROLES

The research found that citizens expected much from their governments. Citizens were clear that the existence of government was essential to a good society. In spite of the influential neo-liberal arguments of the 1980s and 1990s, which sought the rolling back of the state to make way for unbridled market forces, citizens were clear that the state had an indispensable role to play both in the economy and in the wider role of creating a good society. In some parts of the world, the idea of weakening states appeared absurd (Nyerere, 1998).[1]

Citizens wanted state institutions in their countries to be democratic, efficient, effective and strong; capable of standing up to powerful global forces; efficient in the use of public resources; and effective in delivering the public good. At the same time, as we saw in Chapter 4, the study also showed that citizens were dissatisfied and, at times, angry with the present performance of public agencies, officials and institutions.

Citizens wanted a blend of government that was strong in the sense of being efficient, effective and responsive. Citizens also identified three main roles for the state. Each will now be addressed in turn.

Provider

For a large majority of citizens, the role of the state should be that of provider of essential laws, services, frameworks and environments that form the basis for meeting basic needs. Citizens who felt vulnerable and insecure wanted the state to provide policies, programmes and projects to underpin living and to ensure secure livelihoods for all.

What governments needed to provide varied according to different contexts. For tribespeople in India and indigenous peoples in the Pacific, providing meant access to natural resources (such as land, forests and water) for their living and occupations. For rural artisans and small farmers in Africa, Asia and the Caribbean, it meant ensuring low costs, reasonable returns and an efficient market infrastructure. For young people in cities such as Kingston, Nairobi, Dhaka, Sydney and Suva, it implied employment policies and opportunities that brought growth in jobs and maintained living wages. For women in Sri Lanka, New Zealand, South Africa, Barbados and the UK, it took the form of cheap credit, access to markets and child-care facilities. Whatever the context in which citizens lived, they expected the state to be a sensitive, flexible and resourceful *provider*:

The state needs to help rural communities find markets for their agricultural products (a church leader in Vanuatu).

The government should provide children with a good education and ensure that they get work when they finish school (a Tanzanian citizen).

The government should be responsible for funding infrastructure and services (a self-employed man in Niue).

The state should be our father or mother and take responsibility to protect us (a citizen with a disability in Botswana).

The state should ensure the respect of law and security of its citizens (a citizen in Cameroon).

Citizens not only expected state institutions to be providers of basic services, but to do so efficiently, effectively and equitably. What they wanted was a supply of drinking water throughout the year; primary schools with good teachers, buildings and learning aids; physically, socially and economically accessible primary health-care facilities with regular attendance of medical and paramedical staff; the availability of basic medicines and efficient referral services; functioning and properly maintained toilets, sewerage and sanitation facilities; roads that are passable throughout the year; public transport that is affordable, safe and does not feel like an animal carriage; street lighting; systems of irrigation that neither dry up nor flood; capacity for storing, transporting and selling produce; access to credit; infrastructure for shelter; a fair, quick and efficient judicial system; and safety in public spaces.

The state should provide basic social services, such as food, shelter, health care, education (respondents in Guyana, Uganda, Tanzania, Zimbabwe, Fiji).

The state should set up a social security system for the destitute (respondents in Fiji, Trinidad and Tobago, Solomon Islands).

The state should provide infrastructure: roads, houses and hospitals, electricity, etc (respondents in Botswana, Uganda).

Underpinning much of the concern about basic needs was the issue of poverty. A widespread view among citizens was that the state should resolutely address the prevalence of poverty through appropriate measures, such as ensuring 'economic emancipation of people through poverty-alleviation policies and programmes' (respondents in Botswana, Naura and Niue).

A further important strand of meeting basic needs was that the state should provide physical protection to its citizens. This differed in places according to the prevalence of local threats. The incidence of crime, for example, was so high in some countries that the highest priority should be, to quote a citizen from Botswana, 'to restore and maintain peace, order and stability'. The emergence of the 'narco-economy' in the Caribbean, where drug trafficking was associated with crime and violence, presented a significant focus for discontent among citizens who felt that governments should act to eliminate these dark forces.

In addition to physical protection, the need for legal protection was also paramount. Equality before the law was imperative:

There should be no ruling for the rich and no ruling for the poor (respondents in Kenya, Uganda).

The state should provide security for all, without discrimination (respondents in Kenya, Samoa, Malawi).

The state should ensure the rule of law, respect human rights (respondents in Zimbabwe, Papua New Guinea, Tonga).

The state should provide reconciliation [and] should stop the war (respondents in Sri Lanka).

Women said that the state should guarantee their basic human rights:

Ensure property rights of women and legal support for women (respondents in Guyana, Botswana).

Protect women against violence in and outside the home (respondents in Guyana, Sri Lanka, India, New Zealand).

Condemn harmful practices such as genital mutilation of women (respondents in Gambia, Sierra Leone).

Similarly, the law should be free from race bias:

Do away with 'politics of ethnicity' (respondents in Kenya, Fiji Islands, Guyana).

In some parts of the Commonwealth, states took their responsibility to provide seriously and were doing the best they could in difficult circumstances; in other cases, state provision worked only for some citizens – including those who were rich, influential and favoured by the political 'in-crowd'. Citizens in this study asked for equitable provision.

Facilitator

There was widespread acceptance of the view that the state could not, on its own, bring about a good society. Citizens suggested that they had a significant role to play. To make this happen, citizens suggested that state institutions should extend their role beyond that of provider to that of facilitator. Citizen leaders were most vocal about this:

Citizens will not play any righteous roles unless the government shows some sort of love for the poorer class and stands for truth and right (a citizen in Guyana).

> *The state is charged with safekeeping and distribution of resources to the different groups of people...the state only plays an enabling role* (a university professor in Botswana).

> *To enable, support, facilitate, not to impede, not to block [but] to lead and guide, but only after listening; the state should not be preoccupied with command and control* (a citizen in Zimbabwe).

The leitmotif of facilitation was to help and encourage citizens to undertake collective action in their communities. Such action would strengthen the forces of association in communities who, as we saw in Chapter 4, were commonly in a state of disrepair. Particularly important goals for citizen action included renewing the best aspects of culture and heritage, as well as promoting greater caring and sharing between different people in society.

Citizens suggested that state agencies and public officials should facilitate citizen action not just through their policies, programmes and allocation of resources, but through their attitudes and behaviour. The state should see collective citizen endeavour and citizen leadership as assets, not as embarrassments or threats.

In many countries, it was common for citizens to suggest that the state saw citizen activism as a threat. This view was particularly common among those citizens who had definite ideas about how state affairs should be conducted and who had made their views known. Overt reprisals by the state have taken such forms as the curtailment of the freedom of speech, rights to assembly and the freedom of the press:

> *Silence is the greatest threat to a society; but in small communities like ours, you will pay the price of speaking out* (influential citizen, Dominica).

In extreme cases, the state resorts to curfews and imprisonment without trial. Covert reprisals include torture and elimination of recalcitrant and unrepentant critics. In Zimbabwe, local people drew horrific pictures of female farm workers being tortured, mutilated and raped when supporters of one party raided their farm compounds allegedly because the farm workers' community supported an opposition party. Such behaviour has forced many citizens into silence.

Others held the dream of a good society where the state would view criticism and innovative ideas as a positive force to be harnessed, and would even guarantee freedom of opinion and speech:

> *The state should go beyond seeing people as a threat [and should] guarantee and safeguard the rights of citizens* (respondents in Guyana, Nigeria, Bangladesh, Pakistan).

> *The state should ensure that the laws do not oppress citizens* (respondents in Sierra Leone, Dominica, Belize).

However, high-status citizens commonly said that this was difficult to realize because the ruling elite tended to see active citizens as threatening, either because they were perceived as competing for political power or because they might uncover corruption or profligacy.

However, many citizens wanted to contribute to their societies and realized that the alternative was a life of perpetual dependence upon the state – a situation that was untenable because the state could not afford it. What they wanted was for the state to treat them like grown-ups, and to promote an environment that was conducive to self-reliance and self-determination:

> *[Provide skills' training colleges to] get our minds off the desperate survival strategies which land us in crime* (Gambian youth).

[Create] a conducive environment [in which] citizens [can] undertake their activities (respondents in Kenya, Zimbabwe, Lesotho, Botswana, Australia).

Support community initiatives materially and technically in crop production and income generation (respondents in Gambia).

Create an enabling environment for NGOs and local investors (respondents in Swaziland, Guyana, Jamaica).

It was clear that many people felt left out of mainstream development programmes that were meant to benefit them. They saw that being a participant was a necessary condition of being a beneficiary:

The state should ensure that all strata of society are involved in the development process (respondents in Guyana, Zimbabwe, Canada, the UK).

Involve people in decision-making (respondents in Sierra Leone, Malaysia).

Ensure that decision-making structures are inclusive of all sectors of society to enable them to play their role effectively (respondents in Gambia, Swaziland).

Open up for other stakeholders to play their role in poverty alleviation (respondents in Botswana).

[Engage in] dialogue with various political and civic groups to ensure that the policies and strategies formulated are relevant to the people's concerns (respondents in Samoa, Tonga, Tanzania).

Implement more concrete and coherent strategies for enhancing women's advancement, in line with international conventions on women (respondents in Gambia).

Sometimes facilitating citizen action would involve structural reform. In many parts of the former colonies, especially in Sub-Saharan Africa, most people were subsistence farmers. In some countries, the post-colonial ruling elite had acquired large farms, while the crowded peasants were forced to overfarm their family plots, degrading the soil in the process. A more equitable land distribution and tenure system was of strategic importance in integrating peasants within the mainstream economy:

The state should address the problem of land tenure urgently (respondents in Fiji, South Africa).

Promoter

Citizens also wanted the state to be a faithful *promoter*. In promoting equal rights and justice, provision was not seen as enough. Governments can and should make policies and laws intended to help citizens. However, policies to support the poor and the weak will mean little unless promoted and implemented effectively. Resources allocated to programmes to provide for needs might well end up being wastefully consumed in the running of state apparatus. Macro-economic and fiscal policies should be framed, promoted and implemented in ways that protect ordinary citizens from the harmful effects of the forces of globalization and privatization. Policies, procedures and laws should be promoted so that they do not just favour a few. Otherwise, the rich will continue to get richer; and individuals close to public institutions and political leadership will benefit proportionately more:

The government makes good policies...but it gets distorted and does not reach the people for whom it is meant (NGO leader in India).

Access to political office has become a gateway to personal wealth, employment for self and one's clan...people are often bought over a few beers, shirts and 'chitenge' materials (a citizen in Zambia).

There should be responsibilities and privileges given to women in planning and development activities (a citizen in the Solomon Islands).

In its promoter role, the government was expected to listen to, and include, citizens in the process of governance. Numerous ideas were mentioned to promote responsive and inclusive governance.

Citizens wanted state institutions, officials and leaders to share information with them. The systems and processes of the democratic state should be publicly visible and accessible. This should be done voluntarily, and not be a response to petitioning from citizens:

The state should sensitize the public on matters that affect their lives (respondents in Gambia).

Such behaviour on the part of the state will go some way to ensuring that the state is held accountable. It is highly desirable for all elected and appointed public officials to be accountable to citizens for all aspects of government. Systems and processes of accountability need to be far more sophisticated, imaginative and permanent than the placing of votes into ballot boxes:

Democracy does not finish when elections are over...members of parliament are still under public scrutiny by accounting to the people and having the people well versed with the decisions taken on their behalf (a citizen in Samoa).

The state should remember that it exists to serve its citizens (respondents in Namibia, Zambia, Kiribati).

Wherever feasible, public affairs and issues particular to a community or locality should be addressed locally by that community. Devolution of decision-making and resource allocation to local bodies will give local citizens greater access and incentive to participate in the business of government:

There are a lot of dissatisfactions among local people. Most of what is being done is from the top. There is hardly any consultation. So the wishes of the leaders get carried out and not the wishes of the people (a citizen in Malaysia).

Public institutions and officials should behave in a *non-partisan* and *non-discriminatory* manner. All citizens, in the study, were regarded as entitled to the benefits of public policies and, as a corollary, all citizens should respect public laws and procedures. Caste, race, gender, religion, ethnicity, language or other social characteristic should never be the basis of discrimination in public life. Similarly, preferential treatment of particular citizens merely because they support the ruling political party or political leaders is unacceptable.

Citizens expected high standards of behaviour from public officials and political leaders. Those in positions of leadership and authority in state institutions were expected to set standards for society. Citizens wanted their leaders to display vision, practise ethical behaviour, demonstrate high levels of personal and professional integrity and serve society as a whole. Citizens wanted strong and moral leadership:

The state should serve as trustee of national and social values (respondents in Lesotho).

Citizens wanted public institutions and officials to communicate with them, to engage them in dialogue on public issues and to include them in the processes of decision-making and implementation. Citizens did not want to be treated as ignorant, passive, self-centred, apathetic or incompetent. They expected to participate in public affairs and to be regularly included and consulted by public agencies, officials and leaders:

It is a strange thing in our country that power and authority are never shared with others (a woman in Pakistan).

These desires, taken together, suggest that citizens want to reclaim ownership of their democracies:

Managere was a good community, we got involved – when we shifted to Onehunga, a separate borough council, it was a smaller and close-knit community. We came to realize that you got a real sense of well-being by being able to walk the whole area in a half a day. You got to know staff, local policemen, teachers. But when government decided to amalgamate boroughs, communities became bigger and people got more isolated. The amalgamation of smaller communities has been detrimental to the community. People have lost their sense of identity. There have been many complaints (a citizen in Aotearoa/New Zealand).

WHAT CITIZENS CAN DO

Although for the most part disillusioned about the condition of their societies, citizens nevertheless wanted to play their part in improving them. While many citizens were unable to articulate their roles in the context of a grand and strategic vision of progress towards a good society, they generally wanted to play some part, however small and local. While many were feeling downtrodden, downhearted and demoralized, others had at least some confidence and commitment, usually because they had some experience of being engaged in small-scale action. Some were parochial and narrowly self-interested in what actions they were willing to take, while others were more altruistic, spurred on by the selfishness, individualism and 'uncivil' citizen action they saw around them.

Citizens articulated three main roles for themselves. The first role was to be *active citizens* (to demonstrate the virtues of what it is to be a good neighbour). The second role was to engage in *collective citizen action* (to perform voluntary work with others in order to tackle problems). The third was to *participate in political processes* (to play an active role in relation to the state in order to ensure that the state opened itself up to the influence of citizens).

Active citizens

The essence of active citizenship was being a responsible person and acting as a good neighbour. Citizens suggested that this was an important role and involved behaving in ways that exemplify elements of the good society.

Active citizenship should start with an examination of oneself:

> *Citizens need to start by looking into the mirror – criticism starts with an examination of oneself...and then, move into society in general* (a citizen in Jamaica).

It involved owning up to societal responsibilities:

> *Citizens should contribute socially, economically and politically to the welfare of the society in order to make it a good society... They should also obey the law and honour their obligations by paying taxes* (a Kenyan schoolteacher).

It was important to be a good parent and prepare the next generation to behave responsibly in society:

> *I teach my kids to respect elders, send them to religious teachings* (a Fijian woman).

There was widespread acknowledgement that not all citizens were active or responsible. The struggle for survival, selfishness and a lack of interest in the wider problems of society were commonplace:

> *The problem with Malaysians is that we care only for our own problems. If a problem does not concern me I would not do anything* (a youth in Malaysia).

> *Society has got to a stage where we think about ourselves first... I think society has turned rather cynical* (a citizen in the UK).

> *People should reflect introspectively on their character and acknowledge the bad tendencies and immorality in [themselves]* (a citizen in Sierra Leone).

Many citizens wanted to eradicate uncaring, self-centred and uncivil behaviour, and urged people to become more active:

> *There is a pervasive sense of apathy and acceptance of the status quo; ...citizens should understand their role in society and accept responsibility* (a citizens' leader in Trinidad and Tobago).

> *Citizens must adequately participate... Citizens must never get tired* (a public leader in Zimbabwe).

When we were kids you might have been a Girl Guide and you got involved in community things – visiting old people's homes. It was a cool thing to do. Now it's really uncool to be a guide or join some youth group. Let's make it fashionable again (an Australian citizen).

Citizens saw the importance of their own capacities in bringing about a good society, yet they also faced many constraints in being able to play those roles satisfactorily.

Collective citizen action

A second role was acting together with other citizens for the common public good. For most ordinary citizens, the probability of contributing to society increased significantly when they were able to do things together with other citizens. The sum total of limited time, limited energy and limited ability was thought to be a great deal more effective than that of each individual part:

We do voluntary work to build feeder roads, community centres...act as mentors to the young and care for the old and disabled...if we know our rights, we can act as a united force (a Dominican farmer).

A good society is not necessarily without problems, but has the ability to cope with its problems effectively (a farmer in Tobago).

Mutual help and solidarity was perceived as a key part of citizen action:

We can educate the people...train them but in a small group...our Toka group usually works on every Wednesday...it is not only training but creative initiative to work hard, complete the work and reap the fruits (a citizen from Tuvalu Island community).

Today we are taking care of our trees and replace them when they have been eroded or cut down. We also do... donga *rehabilitation and sledge path maintenance by communal effort* (a citizen in Lesotho).

Good organization increased capacity, confidence and cooperation in collective endeavours:

Bati Ndarr women's group has existed for 15 years...it engages in collective communal farming, seed multiplication, literacy, etc (a Gambian woman from the group).

We are small landowners in Jhangr who have organized our efforts at communal farming (a Pakistani peasant).

Citizens' collectives were often effective mobilizers of energies, talent and resources, enabling people to overcome their hesitations and limitations, giving them a sense of power:

The failure of the people in government made us realize we need to look after our own affairs...we built our own school (a Ngomo farmer in Cameroon).

Our organization has great influence on us. Before the organization was formed, we knew nothing and were completely ignorant. The organization has instilled a new soul in us (a woman in Pakistan).

Citizens said that they wanted to be supported by their governments in order to follow such collective action. Both citizens and their leaders agreed that they should contribute to the moulding of society by collaborating in development efforts. This is the vision of a Nigerian citizen:

> *Citizens should engage constructively with the state so as to defend their interests and protect human rights. They should see themselves as architects and builders of a good society by the manner in which they struggle daily to become even more aware of their rights and responsibilities. They should network to demand and protect these rights. They must fight against corruption, both in their lives as well as in the public.*

This brings us to the political dimension of citizenship.

Participate in political processes

Citizens not only wanted to play their own roles in building a good society, but they also wanted a vibrant democracy that allowed and encouraged them to play roles in wider public arenas. The voices of citizens carried a clear message in this respect:

> *A military coup should be seen as a situation in which a family pays and arms a security guard to protect its property and life, only to have the security man turn around to invade the house, take over property and overlordship of the family because the head of the family is deemed to have lost control of the homestead!* (a Nigerian citizen).

> *We have now become the pioneers as the flowing river has run dry. We need to rebuild our lives... I would like my people to unite and stand together and demand our leaders...to be more responsible* (a citizen in Nauru).

> *[The people] must speak out against actions that contradict their principles and beliefs...we have to work hard and*

struggle, take the initiative and organize, and persist in requesting assistance from the government (a citizen in Belize).

People should not let the government rule everything (a citizen in Zimbabwe).

Citizens said that they wanted to engage with public agencies, officials and leaders in order to make their views known, to seek information, to demand accountability and to monitor the policies and programmes of different government agencies and departments. They knew that they could ask their elected officials to answer their queries, but they wanted much more than this. They wanted open government. They knew that to achieve such a state of affairs would require citizens to display tact, perseverance and courage:

A good society is where citizens know their rights, know how to react to violations of those rights (a businessman in Zambia).

We are extremely lucky to have a beautiful island and clever, dynamic people. But we have to find the way to unite and use team work to uplift our country and ourselves (a citizen in Sri Lanka).

CITIZENS' LEADERS

Citizens' leaders played essential roles in enabling and consolidating the contributions of ordinary citizens towards a good society:

We have strong leaders who are honest and have integrity (a Maori youth in Aotearoa/New Zealand).

In the study, citizens repeatedly referred to the inspiration and leadership given by capable and committed citizens' activists, who took a leading role and encouraged the participation and contribution of ordinary citizens in the affairs of their communities. The objectives of these citizens' leaders was to share information, build awareness and mobilize other citizens to become involved. Such citizens enabled, animated, cajoled and facilitated citizen participation and engagement:

- Pai is the leader of the Apolina Urban Workers Association in Samoa. Her group brings together young workers in the village to undertake social and cultural activities. She is able to play the leadership role because her family supports her, and she has been to many training workshops. She recognizes the importance of workers' rights as human rights and is trying to make all members aware of these rights. She wants to promote greater participation of young women workers in the group's activities.
- 'After attending church classes, I went back to my village to organize my people. Elderly people have a lot of knowledge, but they feel marginalized in my village. Literacy classes organized by the church have been very helpful to me in my work in the village' (a slum dweller in Uganda).
- Battilal is a young man in his early 20s living in a slum in Delhi, India. His migrant parents are unskilled labourers in the city. Battilal got a chance to study in a school run by a local NGO. He was encouraged to build a youth group playing *Dholak* (a local drum). Now Battilal's troupe is performing plays to raise awareness of slum dwellers on issues of corruption and health.

Such stories illustrate how ordinary citizens can become leaders, and then promote the participation and engagement of other citizens.

Various factors were identified that helped such citizens' activists to play their valuable leadership roles in society. One was *access to information* about their situation, about government policies and schemes and about emerging opportunities or threats. Another was the opportunity for *wider exposure* beyond their immediate context, so that they could compare their own reality with other contexts, share experiences with other activists and learn about new ways of doing things. A third was *access to training and support structures*, to build their confidence, support their initiative and enterprise, and enhance their strength to undertake action. NGOs often acted as useful intermediaries in encouraging citizen leadership by providing exposure and access to information and training and support.

THE ROLE OF OTHER ACTORS

Citizens were asked to say what other actors might contribute towards a good society. This section describes what they said about NGOs.

In general, NGOs were peripheral to the way in which citizens thought about their societies and how to improve them. NGOs (and cognates such as charities, voluntary organizations, civil society organizations and third-sector organizations) were mentioned in only half of the country reports (24 out of 47).

The subjective importance of NGOs was positively correlated with social class. NGOs were more likely to be seen as important among citizens with high status. NGOs figured much less prominently in the minds of ordinary citizens. For people who were poor, the key issue was survival. What poor people generally wanted was the satisfaction of their basic needs, which were perceived as having three main components: economic security, basic services, and physical security and peace. When ordinary citizens identified external solutions to their problems, they usually selected government as the key agency.

NGOs were significantly more important among people whose basic needs were satisfied. Such people were commonly citizens' leaders or citizens of influence in society. This higher-status group tended to stress the societal importance of association (people's relations with one another through, for example, processes of solidarity or mutual aid) and participation (people's relationship with the political process – for example, by serving on committees or taking part in social movements). Citizens of influence more frequently had the resources, networks, and know-how to help create a good society, and saw NGOs as one means of achieving this.

To evaluate how citizens perceived the role of NGOs, comments about them were rated on a five-point scale, from making a 'very favourable' contribution to society to 'very unfavourable'.

In the 24 countries where NGOs were mentioned, findings were mixed. In fact, the distribution of scores was virtually symmetrical, as shown in Table 5.1.

What were the factors that would contribute to favourable ratings for NGOs and, similarly, to unfavourable ratings?

Three main factors tended to account for more favourable ratings. First, NGOs appeared to be highly regarded when they provided a vehicle for citizen participation in reorganizing society. In Dominica, for example, NGOs were pioneering new and alternative forms of democracy. In the UK, 'citizen organization'

Table 5.1 *Ratings of 24 countries on the contribution of NGOs to a good society*

Very favourable	Favourable	Average	Unfavourable	Very unfavourable
Botswana	Bangladesh	Australia	Ghana	Malawi
Dominica	Canada	Cameroon	Kenya	
	India	Jamaica	Namibia	
	Malaysia	Seychelles	Pakistan	
	New Zealand	Sri Lanka	Gambia	
	Trinidad and Tobago	Swaziland	Tonga	
	UK		Uganda	
			Vanuatu	

was creating broad-base alliances across racial and religious divides to ameliorate the conditions of the inner-city poor. In Canada, indigenous peoples' organizations created a new province. In Trinidad and Tobago, the labour movement, coupled with cooperatives and credit unions, had a strong tradition. The majority populations led the drive for independence in the 1950s. During the 1960s and 1970s, the Black Power movement took hold in Jamaica, and from the 1980s onwards, the women's movement became a powerful force for change. In Bangladesh, NGOs were the only hope in an otherwise corrupt and moribund system. In the circumstances described, NGOs were important touchstones for change – creating movement, life and energy.

Second, NGOs were highly regarded when they provided a focus for cohesion and solidarity. Community and village associations were important, providing local people with a vehicle for their energies and commitments. Such organizations were 'of the people and for the people' and were called community organizations or people's organizations, rather than NGOs. Often, such organizations were so much part of indigenous culture that they were not really seen as associations in any external sense at all. In some parts of the Pacific region, for example, very powerful kinship-based community organizations created a tightly woven network of local relationships that governed social and economic behaviour. At the same time, there was sometimes an overlay of international NGOs who derived their legitimacy from Western norms and finance, which delivered services and development opportunities to islanders. Although less marked, similar divisions between voluntary and community organizations were at work in sophisticated Western economies.

We need to avoid giving an overly romantic picture of the role of community organizations. Traditional associations (based on caste, religion, tribe or ethnic identity) were commonly seen as a mixed blessing. Often, they supported a male view of the world and gave little power or scope to women or young people.

Third, NGOs were well regarded when they were part of development arrangements based on a partnership with the state that yielded progressive outcomes. It was important, in these circumstances, that NGOs retain their independence. Where they were not perceived as independent, as in Uganda or New Zealand, they were criticized.

In terms of the factors that produced unfavourable ratings, the main element was a lack of contact with the people. This factor was mentioned in 11 of the 24 reports (Gambia, Kenya, Malawi, the Seychelles, Swaziland, Pakistan, Malaysia, Ghana, Guyana, Malawi and Vanuatu). Ordinary citizens, particularly the poor, tended to see NGOs as part of an establishment system that was composed of people who already had access to resources.

Second, in some places NGOs were too weak to be effective. This particularly applied to Namibia, Pakistan and Tonga, where capacity was said to be very low. In Vanuatu, NGOs were seen as having little finance and human resources, and were perceived as being run by a loose cadre of activists with little relevance to the concerns of most local people. Lack of clear vision was mentioned as a factor in Cameroon. Wasteful duplication and competition were noted in Ghana.

The third factor was corruption. This was mentioned in several reports. There were two main forms of criticism that might be roughly categorized as 'mild' or 'harsh' criticism. When NGOs were mildly criticized, they were perceived as having and keeping resources for themselves, rather than allowing resources to trickle down to local people. This criticism focused on the use of vehicles, limited access to services and the formation of an 'in-crowd' who helped each other to get a bigger slice of the cake. Harsh criticism implied that people from NGOs were creaming off the top; money meant for beneficiaries was finding its way into the pockets of the providers.

Comparing these findings with other research raises the immediate question of 'whose associational revolution?' This is a reference to Lester Salamon's famous suggestion that the growth in NGOs at the end of the 20th century is comparable to the growth of the nation state at the end of the 19th century (Salamon, 1994). If this is the case, it is clear that the revolution is passing unnoticed by many ordinary citizens. It is a middle-class revolution with apparently little significance lower down the social scale.

Our findings replicate those of the World Bank in their *Voices of the Poor* study. Narayan (2000) notes that the role of NGOs in the lives of the poor is limited, and the poor depend primarily upon their informal networks.[2] Findings from the World Bank study suggest that, given the scale of poverty, NGOs touch relatively few lives, and poor people give NGOs mixed ratings. In some areas, NGOs are the only institutions that people trust, and in some cases they are credited with saving lives. Where there is a strong NGO presence, new partnerships between government and NGOs are beginning to emerge. However, poor people sometimes also report that, besides being rude and forceful, NGO staff members are poor listeners. The poor report that they consider some NGOs to be largely irrelevant, self-serving, limited in their outreach and also corrupt, although to a much lesser extent than the state. There are relatively few cases of NGOs who have invested in reorganizing the poor in order to change poor people's bargaining power relative to markets or the state. Because the current study was conducted in some countries with the world's largest NGOs (some of which also comprised the world's most successful NGOs), there are important lessons to be learned. The main message, however, is still one of scale – even the larger and most successful NGOs may not reach the majority of poor households. This chimes in with other criticisms of NGOs as delivery vehicles for development (Bhargave and Bhat, 2000; Smillie, 1995; Edwards, 2000).

FACTORS THAT HELP AND HINDER

In some respects, it appears that, for some citizens, NGOs were as remote as governments. This prompts the question: what are the mechanisms that can connect citizens with the wider society? What will mediate the relationship between citizens and the wider world? Before answering that question (see Chapter 6 for a full discussion), we need to ask an essential preliminary question: what are the factors that help or hinder citizen engagement?

We have seen from the data that persistent faith in one's inability to change circumstances is a significant inhibitor of citizen action. Many people saw government as the only hope, even when all the evidence suggested that government was part of the problem. Moreover, the fact that many people were struggling to meet their basic needs of food, clothing and shelter compounded this. Many people were so preoccupied with the basics of life that they had no time, energy, capacity or, indeed, wherewithal to confront the forces that oppressed them. They lacked the basic means to do so (money, access to paper, telephones, technical know-how, knowledge of the system, connections to people with power, and so on) – means that are taken for granted by the middle-class professional. Among marginal and poor communities, lack of resources, combined with dependency, alienation and apathy, were powerful counters to any sense of positive change. In some communities, there were social or ethnic divisions that made collective action almost impossible. Moreover, any sense of reward for efforts was remote and long term, whereas people tended to experience their problems here and now.

In some countries, as we have seen, activism of any kind is greeted with suspicion by authorities. People were fearful of speaking out against power, since power could squash such criticism with ease unless it was backed up by something more substantial than a moral vision of a good society.

For governments, there appears to be little in it for them to respond to demands for change. Take, for example, the conclusions of a Jamaican committee that was established in April 1999 to consider the aftermath of riots:

If citizens are cut off from, or subordinate to, the authorities [who] make critical decisions affecting their lives; [and] the available means for getting redress are distant and ineffective...[then] this means that government is a power over the people rather than a means through which people exercise their sovereign authority.[3]

This comment is sound and useful, and most democratic thinkers would agree with it. The problem is that governments everywhere, regardless of their presentational rhetoric, have nearly always been driven by forces of oligarchy, rather than democracy; and government leaders and officials tend to enjoy power, whether it is in the interests of a good society or not (Michels, 1911). As we have seen, governments tend to become corrupted when pursuing a narrowly private agenda, rather than acting in the public benefit. This leads to corruption with a small and a capital 'c'. With such corruption, the call for reform falls on even deafer ears because there are too many who benefit from the status quo.

In part, what needs to happen is the reconfiguration of citizens' interests, and the interests of their governments, in order to create a new model of good governance. Indeed, a model for this has emerged from the current study.

GOOD GOVERNANCE

Over the past decade, the importance of governance has been recognized. UN Secretary-General Kofi Annan noted (1998):

UN programmes now target good governance, safeguarding the rule of law, verifying elections, training police, monitoring human rights, fostering investment and promoting accountable administration. Without good governance, no amount of funding, no amount of charity will set the developing world on the path to prosperity.

The World Bank (1992) defined good governance as 'the means in which power is exercised in the management of a country's economic and social resources for development, and good governance is synonymous with sound development management'. The Overseas Development Agency (ODA) identified four components of good governance (ODA, 1993):

- the legitimacy of government, which depends upon the existence of participatory processes and the consent of those who are governed;
- the accountability of both political and official elements of government for their actions, depending upon the availability of information, freedom of the media, transparency of decision-making and the existence of mechanisms to call individual institutions to account;
- the competence of governments to formulate appropriate policies, make timely decisions, implement them effectively and deliver services; and
- respect for human rights and the rule of law to guarantee individual and group rights and security, to produce a framework for economic and social security and to allow and encourage all individuals to participate.

It is clear that all of these definitions and criteria push in the right direction. Unfortunately, these definitions mix descriptive criteria with normative criteria. We suggest 'collective decision-taking and action in which government is one stakeholder among others' as a descriptive definition of 'governance'. We suggest a normative definition of 'good governance', which is: 'collective decision-taking and action that lead to the common public good'.

The current study reveals an important model of good governance by building on the complementary roles of state and citizens.

BOX 5.1 GOOD GOVERNANCE

Citizens' Roles   **State Roles**

Engaged citizen ◄─────── Participation ──────► Promoter

Collective citizen action ◄─ Association ──────► Facilitator

Active citizens ◄─────────── Basic Needs ──────► Provider

In fulfilling basic needs, the state is expected to play a providing role. Active citizens complement such a providing role by playing their part.

In strengthening associational aspects of society, collective citizen action is the 'actor'. The state complements this with its facilitator role, which is crucial to building and nurturing collective citizen action.

In enhancing the participation of citizens, the state has to play the role of an active promoter. By engaging themselves in the public arena, citizens complement the 'promoter role' of the state.

A crucial thread in encouraging and sustaining the various roles of citizens is the citizens' leader. Such citizens' leaders need recognition, encouragement and support from the state in order to strengthen their leadership roles in society. How this is put into practice is the topic of the following chapter.

CHAPTER 6

What is to be Done?

We have now become pioneers as the flowing river has run dry. We need to rebuild our lives... I would like my people to unite and stand together and demand that our leaders ...be more responsible (a citizen in Nauru).

What is the central message from this study? In the minds of citizens, it is simple. A good society boils down to meeting the requirements for basic needs, association and participation.

For citizens, governance should be about meeting these three conditions. However, the current view of governance, as described in Chapter 1, has taken little account of the needs of citizens. It developed from the perspective of a Washington elite and gives undue prominence to wealth creation, seeing the market as master rather than as servant. The present study suggests that for ordinary citizens, once basic needs have been satisfied, other factors – notably, associating with other people and taking part in public affairs – become more important.

For citizens, the public domain – whether through state or voluntary action – is of primary importance. However, according to the current consensus, private action – through the global market – is of principal importance. It is small wonder that governments are out of step with what their citizens want. If citizens' needs are to be met – and in democratic societies the wishes of citizens are sovereign – it will be necessary to change the current consensus to a new consensus.

Table 6.1 *The old and new consensus*

	Old consensus	New consensus
State	Weak and withering	Strong and sensitive
Market	Master	Servant
Civil society	Intermediary organizations lead	Citizens and their organizations lead

A NEW CONSENSUS

Table 6.1 contrasts the new consensus with the current consensus. To create the new consensus, we have to fulfill three conditions:

- a strong state and a strong civil society;
- a 'deepened' democracy and democratic culture;
- an enlarged role for citizens.

Let us take each of these in turn.

STRONG STATE; STRONG CIVIL SOCIETY

Citizens regard the state and civil society as equally important and, in their view, both need to be strong. For citizens the state and civil society are complementary, while for the Washington elite they are alternatives, with civil society expanding to fill the space as the state shrinks. The core of a new consensus would be to give state and civil society parity in which each is strong and complementary.

What kind of strong state do citizens want? Citizens want efficient and effective performance from their governments. They want public institutions to ensure that basic needs are met through the provision of essential services. They want the state to encourage associational life, so that citizens can play a full part in delivering public goods. They want the state to encourage political participation, and to take steps to ensure human rights, social justice and other requisites of a civilized state.

These are tall expectations. The state not only needs to be strong but also sensitive. It needs to perform multiple roles – of provider, facilitator and promoter. The state needs to walk along a narrow path flanked by two dangerous crevasses. On the left there is the risk of falling into behaviour that is dominating, totalitarian, hegemonic and centralized. On the right there is the risk of falling into behaviour that is *laissez faire*, shrunken and powerless to control the market. To walk the path involves a difficult balancing act; yet, if citizens' needs are to be satisfied, this is what the state must do.

And what do citizens expect of themselves? Citizens have equally high expectations of themselves. They say that they want to be aware and informed; understand their rights and responsibilities; behave as active citizens in the family and community; show solidarity, generosity and mutual support towards fellow citizens; participate in local associations and organizations in order to work on a common public agenda; demonstrate assertive, caring and ethical leadership; and connect with public institutions, officials and leaders on public concerns. Citizens will, therefore, avoid passivity, apathy and self-centredness.

The model that emerges is based on rights and responsibilities. This takes us right back to the early pioneers of democratic theory, when basic agreements about rights and responsibilities, called the 'social contract' or the 'covenant', were the foundation of civilized political society (Selbourne, 1994).

DEEPENING DEMOCRACY

Once the fundamentals of rights and responsibilities are accepted as part of a new consensus of strong state and strong civil society, it is possible to make progress towards participatory democracy.

In the past century or so, the growth of democracy has tended to mean the growth of representative democracy. This has involved elections, representatives, political parties, elected parliaments and legislatures, an independent judiciary and a non-partisan executive. Beyond these institutions and processes, representative democracy also requires just, open and honest government, respect for the rule of the law and regard for human rights (including the rights of women, children, disabled people, indigenous peoples and minorities).

As we have seen from the study, such representative democracy is no longer enough. Citizens want a deepening of democracy to make it more direct and participatory. Such a deepening of democracy requires action both on the demand side of governance (what citizens do) and on the supply side of governance (what the state does). Such action needs to be comprehensive, embracing attitudes, behaviour, processes and structures. The goal of this action should be to close the gap between the demand and supply, so that governance is, as far as possible, seamless between 'consumers' and 'creators'.

To close the gap on the demand side, citizens need to display activism, leadership, association, commitment and engagement. In the new consensus, democracy would not be a spectator sport, with citizens merely applauding or sighing from the sidelines, or forced into adversarial complaint or criticism. Participatory democracy would be conducted in an arena where the common public good is negotiated, intense deliberation and dialogue take place and diversity is celebrated. The sport is less about who wins or loses, and more about who takes part.

To close the gap on the supply side, governments need to value the opinions and experiences of all citizens – old and young, rich and poor, men and women, people from all castes, creeds and groups. Acknowledging and valuing talent, wisdom, capacity and commitment among all women, men and children is a key ingredient. Bridging the gap also means listening to contrary opinions and perspectives, openly debating conflicting positions and interests, and seeking consensual agreements as well as negotiated settlements. It means valuing diversity while building agreements on common ground. Above all, it means accepting and welcoming criticism, seeing it as a sign of a healthy society.

Such an approach will require innovation and initiative on the part of state institutions, public officials and political leaders. Special efforts will be required in order to share information, build transparency and enable participation. Commonwealth governments have already gone a long way down this route, starting with the *Harare Declaration* in 1991, the Millbrook Action Programme in 1995, to the 1999 *Fancourt Declaration on Globalization and People-Centred Development*. A logical corollary to these declarations – reproduced in the form of Appendices 1, 2 and 3 at the end of this book – would be to add statements about the intent to 'deepen' democracy.

If they do this, democratic states will regain much of the legitimacy that they have lost.

ENLARGING CITIZENS' ACTIONS

If the new consensus is to work, it will be vital for citizens to play a greater role in the public domain. The number of players involved in governance has to increase, otherwise the many will always be ruled by the few. A necessary condition of a good society is an active society.

The traditional way of thinking about engagement in civil society is through people's participation in NGOs. Evidence to support the importance of this endeavour is mixed. On the one hand, Lester Salamon observes an 'associational revolution' in which a new third force of citizens' power is at work (Salamon, 1994). On the other hand, Robert Putnam suggests that people are in retreat from collective organizations so that people's influence and interest in the public domain are decreasing (Putnam, 2000). However, this apparent paradox can be resolved. Whereas organized and registered NGOs appear to be in a stage of rapid growth, the current study suggests that this is a middle-class phenomenon and is not spread evenly throughout society.

The present study shows that citizens regard their own organizations, which might be called citizens' organizations, as far more important than NGOs. NGOs are often perceived as being remote, much like governments. Data in the study show that people will develop their own organizations, providing that the role of these organizations is to achieve benefits that are directly related to the people and their communities. People value action that solves their problems; so long as this happens, they will sustain the action through their own energies and resources. This activity is best described as 'organizing' rather than 'organization', since activity is based upon local affiliations of family, kinship, caste, religion or ethnicity, rather than upon a formal structure or constitution. Such informal activity forms the bedrock of civil society, though it is hard for outsiders to detect, to count or to evaluate it in other ways.

This activity is different from that found among NGOs, trade unions, cooperatives and other formal, voluntary, independent and intermediary organizations. To engage citizens and their organizations, it is important to reach below the level of NGOs, where resources have been directed, and to reach citizens and their organizations. Moreover, in order to engage their interest, it is of little use to appeal to citizens' sense of honour or altruism. A more powerful incentive is appeal to their self-interest and to show them ways in which they may increase their power.

PROBABLE FUTURES

Thus far in this chapter we have set out a series of ideals based on the desires of citizens. A glimpse at the empirical data in Chapter 4, however, might be sufficient to shatter these ideals as romantic illusions. Throughout the study, in all countries of the Commonwealth, citizens emphasized that governments were failing to meet their needs. Due to a lack of resources, governments were no longer providing essential services. Some regimes were repressive, were pursuing violent conflict, were corrupt, or had otherwise lost their way. Even so-called progressive democracies were said to be merely muddling along and in need of renewal. The state of the world, for the most part, is the opposite of what citizens want.

Moreover, according to some individuals, the world is set to get worse. The CIA has forecast the state of the world in the year 2015 (Central Intelligence Agency, 2000). Although economic growth is set to continue, the gap between the rich and the burgeoning middle class, on the one hand, and the poor and dispossessed, on the other, will continue to increase. The United States will thrive economically and will continue to be the single dominant power in the world. Yet the outlook for many parts of the world is bleak. Worst affected will be Sub-Saharan Africa, where problems will multiply as a result of AIDS, pushing the region into economic free fall and leading to a spiral of humanitarian crises and military conflicts. The Middle East is set to remain locked in conflict with almost no prospects of breaking the logjam, and with marked economic deterioration a certain outcome. The Eurasian landmass, from parts of Eastern Europe, to the Caucasus, through to Central Asia, faces dim economic prospects. So, too, does most of Latin America, save for Mexico and the cone of South America. Despite the recent collapse, prospects for South-East Asia are better, though Japan will have to face up to its pronounced economic difficulties and the challenge of an ageing population. Europe may fare well, providing it can find a way to manage large numbers of dependent people through demographic trends. India and China are both on the rise and are set to play a greater regional and global role, though both have issues of governance to face and may experience civil disorder due to the increased gap between the rich and poor.

This analysis suggests a world even more polarized than now. Not surprisingly, then, the forecast is also for greater discontent. Disaffection may find expression through more 'rogue states', increased international terrorism and a growth in crime. The spread of weapons of mass destruction may, along with environmental degradation, financial turbulence and conflicts over water shortages in large tracts of the globe, produce a still more volatile world than the present one.

This strong dose of 'realism' from the CIA should be enough to temper the sense of 'idealism' of the first section of this chapter. One lesson that history provides is that concepts of morality, and the pursuit of ideals, are a weak force and they tend to take second place to the cut and thrust of ambition and self-interest. This might lead us to the position of the realists we described in Chapter 1, for whom the weight of current circumstances nullifies ambitions for positive change. In the words of Isagani R Serrano (1999):

That's the way the world was, is and will be. There's not much we can do to change it.

Perhaps we should all give up.

And yet, human beings appear blessed with a sense of being able to change things for the better. Take Marx and Engels, who produced the *Communist Manifesto* in 1848. The social and political circumstances within Europe were far worse then than they are now. Marx and Engels still produced a document that shaped history (though not in the way that they would have liked). People continue to produce such visions of the future. For example, Wright (2001) has recently produced a *Community Manifesto*. This document has a similar title and a virtually identical vision to that of Marx and Engels – namely, to create an equal society where people cooperate with each other, free from domination by the state. Edwards (1999) has stressed the importance of being positive. He has not shrunk from pointing out the errors of the past and drawing attention to the obstacles to a positive future. But he remains optimistic, nevertheless. Rather than dreaming about utopia, or seeking out a magic bullet to make it all right, he urges us to get down to work to make it better. Even the CIA acknowledges that, with better governance, its depressing scenario could be immeasurably improved.

Yes, but how? How can we act meaningfully and influence events so that we can obtain more positive futures?

We have to recognize that, despite half a century of development, we have very little to show for it. Many good intentions have not worked out in practice. The reasons for this vary. Some initiatives have been poorly designed. Others have been too weak to combat huge global forces. In other cases, initiatives have been aimed at the wrong targets. Sometimes, they have been subverted to fulfil the agenda of the implementing agency rather than its beneficiaries. In other cases, money has gone into the wrong hands. There is an almost inexhaustible list of what can and has gone wrong. There are few success stories in the literature upon which to build a new model.

Indeed, social scientists have found it far easier to document interventions that have failed rather than list those that have succeeded. This phenomenon is sometimes known as the 'nothing works hypothesis' because research studies of many worthy interventions have produced negative, neutral or, at best, lukewarm results (Ball and Knight, 1988). The result is that social scientists have been unable to create testable theories that link inputs to processes, outputs and desirable outcomes. It follows that there are few guides to good practice in intervention; and those that purport to be so tend to be based upon unevaluated fashion rather than hard-headed empirical evidence.

The prevalence of the 'nothing works hypothesis' partly explains why there is such a gap between social theory and practice. Social scientists have found it difficult to create conditions where they can describe problems and locate practical interventions that solve these problems. As a result, much social science gets stuck at the level of problems; and when recommendations are made, they are more likely to be based upon hope than upon evidence. Indeed, as we saw in Chapter 1, the current consensus on governance is that it is nothing more than a 'myth driven by a powerful elite' (Edwards, 1999).

DESIRABLE FUTURES

There is an urgent need to learn about how we can improve governance. Governance has become something of a buzzword, and there is a growing literature about how to do it (Agere, 2000). Much of this literature focuses on technical assistance to the supply side of institutional reform. However, recent practice suggests that to make governance work effectively, it is necessary to bring in the demand side of governance – namely, citizens and their organizations – and to work on supply and demand together (Cornwall and Gaventa, 2001). Intervention needs to be holistic and systemic, conveying the sources of formal power closer to the people. This brings us to the notion of participatory governance, defined here as 'the process of collective decision-making in the public domain where government is one stakeholder among others and citizens affected by decisions are included' (Hague et al, 1998).

Before this can happen, the stakeholders need to be able to talk to each other. It is crucial that the language used in civil society development is precise. At present, the sphere is plagued with fuzzy and imprecise terminology that makes it hard for people to understand one another, and acts as a strong barrier to progress. Many conferences issue vague and woolly *communiqués* that lead nowhere. Before significant and useful dialogue can take place, all actors must use the same commonly agreed terms.

There is an urgent need to develop tools that will make participatory governance a reality. On the supply side, tools include governance audits in which experts help a government to think through its approach to becoming more open and participatory. On the demand side, there is a need to encourage a range of participatory ventures that develop 'citizens' voices' at a subaltern level in society – operating where traditional NGOs cannot normally reach. Such ventures should be undertaken in a spirit of exploration and adventure.

Again, there is an obligation to pioneer new methods of evaluating actions of this kind that are participatory and statistically rigorous. One such opportunity is to develop the theory of personal constructs invented by George Kelly (1955). These techniques contain the potential to extend the capability of participatory evaluation techniques, assigning numerical codes to outputs, producing scores that can be manipulated statistically. As well as yielding precise information on outputs, this methodology has the potential to identify which interventions produce which kinds of results under what conditions. The dissemination of results through academic journals, the internet, the news media and conferences would provide cogent and convincing evidence to policy-makers that participatory governance is not just a piece of wishful thinking.

Furthermore, interventions of this kind must be cued into existing positive social movements, such as those that improve the environment, raise the status of women, increase the power of indigenous peoples and counter racism and other forms of oppression. Part of what is important about such movements is that they challenge the status quo. More importantly, they also replace 'masculine' ways of organizing through order, hierarchy, competition, objectivity and compartmentalization with 'feminine' ways of 'going with the flow', reciprocity, cooperation, subjectivity and inclusivity. If the world is to make progress, then this type of organizing is necessary – as many people suggest. Part of the agenda is to build a new consciousness.

Such a consciousness could lead to a coalition of interests that would implement new models of participatory governance, acting on the hearts and minds of those who, at present, are less sympathetic to a new people-based consensus to replace the Washington consensus of the 1990s.

The creation of a new consciousness about participatory governance, the development of interventions that help to produce it and new methods that evaluate these interventions, the dissemination of results through channels of influence – these elements, in combination, may produce a new people- and evidence-based consensus about how we develop the world.

1

Harare Commonwealth Declaration (1991)

The Commonwealth Heads of Government Meeting (CHOGM) in Harare in 1991 reaffirmed each country's confidence in the Commonwealth as a voluntary association of sovereign independent states. Each country is responsible for its own policies, consulting and cooperating in the interests of its peoples, and promoting international understanding and world peace.

Members of the Commonwealth include people of many different races and origins, encompass every state of economic development, and comprise a rich variety of cultures, traditions and institutions.

The special strength of the Commonwealth lies in the combination of the diversity of its members, with their shared inheritance in language, culture and the rule of law. The Commonwealth way is to seek consensus through consultation and the sharing of experience. It is uniquely placed to serve as a model and as a catalyst for new forms of friendship and cooperation to all in the spirit of the Charter of the United Nations.

Its members also share a commitment to certain fundamental principles. These were set out in a *Declaration of Commonwealth Principles* agreed by predecessors at the CHOGM in Singapore in 1971. Those principles have stood the test of time, and the *Harare Declaration* reaffirms its full and continuing commitment to these principles. In particular, Commonwealth members today (as 20 years ago):

- believe that international peace and order, global economic development and the rule of international law are essential to the security and prosperity of mankind;
- believe in the liberty of the individual under the law, in equal rights for all citizens regardless of gender, race, colour, creed or political belief, and in the individual's inalienable right to participate by means of free and democratic political processes in framing the society in which he or she lives;
- recognize racial prejudice and intolerance as a dangerous sickness and a threat to healthy development, and racial discrimination as an unmitigated evil;
- oppose all forms of racial oppression and are committed to the principles of human dignity and equality;
- recognize the importance and urgency of economic and social development to satisfy the basic needs and aspirations of the vast majority of the peoples of the world, and seek the progressive removal of the wide disparities in living standards amongst our members.

In Harare, the purpose of Commonwealth members has been to apply those principles in the contemporary situation as the Commonwealth prepares to face the challenges of the 1990s and beyond.

Internationally, the world is no longer locked in the iron grip of the Cold War. Totalitarianism is giving way to democracy and justice in many parts of the world. Decolonization is largely complete. Significant changes are at last underway in South Africa. These changes, so desirable and heartening in themselves, present the world and the Commonwealth with new tasks and challenges.

During the last 20 years, several Commonwealth countries have made significant progress in economic and social development.

There is increasing recognition that commitment to market principles and openness to international trade and investment can promote economic progress and improve living standards. Many Commonwealth countries are poor and face acute problems, including excessive population growth, crushing poverty, debt burdens and environmental degradation. More than half of the member states are particularly vulnerable because of their very small societies.

Only sound and sustainable development can offer these millions of individuals the prospect of betterment. Achieving this will require a flow of public and private resources from the developed to the developing world, and domestic and international regimes must be conducive to realizing these goals. Development facilitates the task of tackling a range of problems that affect the whole global community, such as environmental degradation, the problems of migration and refugees, the fight against communicable diseases and drug production and trafficking.

Having reaffirmed the principles to which the Commonwealth is committed, and reviewed the problems and challenges which the world, and the Commonwealth as part of it, face, Commonwealth members pledge the Commonwealth and its countries to work with renewed vigour, concentrating especially in the following areas:

1   the protection and promotion of the fundamental political values of the Commonwealth:
    • democracy, democratic processes and institutions that reflect national circumstances; the rule of law and the independence of the judiciary; just and honest government;
    • fundamental human rights, including equal rights and opportunities for all citizens regardless of race, colour, creed or political belief;
2   equality for women, so that they may exercise their full and equal rights;

3   provision of universal access to education for the population of Commonwealth countries;

4   continuing action to bring about the end of Apartheid and the establishment of a free, democratic, non-racial and prosperous South Africa;

5   the promotion of sustainable development and the alleviation of poverty in the countries of the Commonwealth through:

- a stable international economic framework within which growth can be achieved;
- sound economic management, recognizing the central role of the market economy;
- effective population policies and programmes;
- sound management of technological change;
- the freest possible flow of multilateral trade on terms that are fair and equitable to all, taking account of the special requirements of developing countries;
- an adequate flow of resources from the developed to developing countries, and action to alleviate the debt burdens of developing countries most in need;
- the development of human resources – in particular, through education, training, health, culture, sport and programmes for strengthening family and community support – paying special attention to the needs of women, youth and children;

6   effective and increasing programmes of bilateral and multilateral cooperation aimed at raising living standards;

7   extending the benefits of development within a framework of respect for human rights;

8   the protection of the environment through respect for the principles of sustainable development, which were enunciated at Langkawi;

9   action to combat drug trafficking and abuse and communicable diseases;

10   help for small Commonwealth states in tackling their particular economic and security problems;

11 support for the United Nations and other international institutions in the world's search for peace, disarmament and effective arms control; and in the promotion of international consensus on major global political, economic and social issues.

To give weight and effectiveness to these commitments, member states intend to focus and improve Commonwealth cooperation in these areas. This would include strengthening the capacity of the Commonwealth to respond to requests from members for assistance in entrenching the practices of democracy, accountable administration and the rule of law.

Member states call on all the intergovernmental institutions of the Commonwealth to seize the opportunities presented by these challenges. Member states pledge to assist them to develop programmes that harness shared historical, professional, cultural and linguistic heritage and that complement the work of other international and regional organizations.

Member states invite the Commonwealth Parliamentary Association and non-governmental Commonwealth organizations to play their full part in promoting these objectives, in a spirit of cooperation and mutual support.

In reaffirming the principles of the Commonwealth and in committing to pursuing them in policy and action, in response to the challenges of the 1990s, in areas where member states believe that the Commonwealth has a distinctive contribution to offer, the Heads of Government express a determination to renew and enhance the value and importance of the Commonwealth as an institution which can, and should, strengthen and enrich the lives not only of its own members and their peoples but also of the wider community of peoples of which they are a part.

Would you like to know more about the Commonwealth? Why not visit our website at www.thecommonwealth.org. Or phone, fax or write to us at:

Commonwealth Secretariat
Information and Public Affairs Division
Marlborough House
Pall Mall, London SW1Y 5HX, UK
Tel: +44 (0)20 7747 6385/86; Fax: +44 (0)20 7839 9081
Email: info@commonwealth.int

Source: originally published by the Information and Public Affairs Division
(1998)

Millbrook Commonwealth Action Programme on the Harare Declaration (1995)

The Commonwealth is an association of 54 countries around the world, sharing many common interests and a set of basic principles. These principles are enshrined in the 1991 *Harare Commonwealth Declaration*. This landmark agreement set the association on a new course of promoting democracy and good government, human rights and the rule of law, gender equality, and sustainable economic and social development.

At their 1995 summit in New Zealand, Commonwealth Heads of Government Meeting (CHOGM) adopted a Commonwealth Action Programme to fulfil more effectively their commitment to the Harare principles. This programme took the name of the place where leaders met and adopted the programme: Millbrook. The programme is in three parts. It advances Commonwealth fundamental political values, promotes sustainable development and facilitates consensus-building. Heads of Government also established a mechanism – a Ministerial Action Group of Foreign Ministers (CMAG) – to address serious and persistent violations of these principles. What follows is the full text of the Millbrook Commonwealth Action Programme.

MILLBROOK COMMONWEALTH ACTION PROGRAMME ON THE HARARE DECLARATION

12 November 1995

1   At Harare in 1991, we pledged to work for the protection and promotion of the fundamental political values of the association, namely democracy, democratic processes and institutions which reflect national circumstances, fundamental human rights, the rule of law and the independence of the judiciary, and just and honest government. We agreed at the same time to work for the promotion of socio-economic development, recognizing its high priority for most Commonwealth countries. During our Retreat at Millbrook, we decided to adopt a Commonwealth Action Programme to fulfil more effectively the commitments contained in the *Harare Commonwealth Declaration*. This Programme is in three parts:
*   advancing Commonwealth fundamental political values;
*   promoting sustainable development; and
*   facilitating consensus building.

1: ADVANCING COMMONWEALTH FUNDAMENTAL POLITICAL VALUES

Measures in support of processes and institutions for the practice of the Harare Principles

2   The Secretariat should enhance its capacity to provide advice, training and other forms of technical assistance to governments in promoting the Commonwealth's fundamental political values, including:
*   assistance in creating and building the capacity of requisite institutions;
*   assistance in constitutional and legal matters, including with selecting models and initiating programmes of democratization;

- assistance in the electoral field, including the establishment or strengthening of independent electoral machinery, civic and voter education, the preparation of Codes of Conduct, and assistance with voter registration;
- observation of elections, including by-elections or local elections where appropriate, at the request of the member governments concerned;
- strengthening the rule of law and promoting the independence of the judiciary through the promotion of exchanges among, and training of, the judiciary;
- support for good government, particularly in the area of public service reform; and
- other activities, in collaboration with the Commonwealth Parliamentary Association and other bodies, to strengthen the democratic culture and effective parliamentary practices.

Measures in response to violations of the Harare principles

3   Where a member country is perceived to be clearly in violation of the *Harare Commonwealth Declaration*, and particularly in the event of an unconstitutional overthrow of a democratically elected government, appropriate steps should be taken to express the collective concern of Commonwealth countries and to encourage the restoration of democracy within a reasonable time frame. These include:
- immediate public expression by the Secretary-General of the Commonwealth's collective disapproval of any such infringement of the Harare principles;
- early contact by the Secretary-General with the *de facto* government, followed by continued good offices and appropriate technical assistance to facilitate an early restoration of democracy;
- encouraging bilateral *demarchés* by member countries, especially those within the region, both to express disapproval and to support early restoration of democracy;

- appointment of an envoy or a group of eminent Commonwealth representatives where, following the Secretary-General's contacts with the authorities concerned, such a mission is deemed beneficial in reinforcing the Commonwealth's good offices role;
- stipulation of up to two years as the time frame for the restoration of democracy where the institutions are not in place to permit the holding of elections within, say, a maximum of six months;
- pending restoration of democracy, exclusion of the government concerned from participation at ministerial-level meetings of the Commonwealth, including Commonwealth Heads of Government Meetings (CHOGMs);
- suspension of participation at all Commonwealth meetings and of Commonwealth technical assistance if acceptable progress is not recorded by the government concerned after a period of two years; and
- consideration of appropriate further bilateral and multilateral measures by all member states (eg limitation of government to government contacts; people-to-people measures; trade restrictions; and, in exceptional cases, suspension from the association) to reinforce the need for change in the event that the government concerned chooses to leave the Commonwealth and/or persists in violating the principles of the *Harare Commonwealth Declaration* even after two years.

Mechanism for implementation of measures

4 We have decided to establish a Commonwealth Ministerial Action Group on the *Harare Declaration* in order to deal with serious or persistent violations of the principles contained in that Declaration. The Group will be convened by the Secretary-General and will comprise the Foreign Ministers of eight

countries,* supplemented as appropriate by one or two additional ministerial representatives from the region concerned. It will be the Group's task to assess the nature of the infringement and recommend measures for collective Commonwealth action aimed at the speedy restoration of democracy and constitutional rule.

5   The composition, terms of reference and operation of the Group will be reviewed by us every two years.

2: PROMOTING SUSTAINABLE DEVELOPMENT

6   We reaffirmed our view that the Commonwealth should continue to be a source of help in promoting development and literacy and in eradicating poverty, particularly as these bear on women and children. With a view to enhancing its capacity in this area, we agreed on the following steps:

- to strengthen the Secretariat's capacity for undertaking developmental work through support for its various Funds and especially by restoring the resources of the Commonwealth Fund for Technical Cooperation (CFTC) to their 1991–1992 level in real terms; and to provide adequate resources to the Commonwealth of Learning and to the Commonwealth Foundation;
- to support a greater flow of investment to developing member countries through such schemes as the Commonwealth Private Investment Initiative;
- to work for continued progress in assisting countries with unsustainable debt burdens and to promote enhanced multilateral concessional financial flows to developing countries; in particular, to support new and innovative mechanisms for relief on multilateral debt, such as the one

---

* At the 1997 Edinburgh CHOGM, the membership of CMAG was revised. It is currently comprised of ministers from Barbados, the UK, Botswana, Canada, Ghana, Malaysia, New Zealand and Zimbabwe.

proposed by the British Chancellor of the Exchequer at the 1994 Commonwealth Finance Ministers Meeting in Malta, and reiterated subsequently;

- to support the Secretariat in facilitating the adoption by more Commonwealth countries of successful self-help schemes, with non-governmental agencies and others acting as catalytic agents, for mobilizing the energies of people in alleviating poverty;

- to support the efforts of small-island developing states to mitigate the effects on their development of environmental change, natural disasters and the changing international trading system; and

- to combat the spread of HIV/AIDS, which threatens large parts of the younger population of many countries, recognizing that the effective exploitation of economic opportunities requires a healthy and educated population; and to provide further resources to renew the core funding of the Southern African Network of AIDS Organizations (SANASO), along with increased funding for United Nations Children's Fund (UNICEF) initiatives in Southern Africa.

3: FACILITATING CONSENSUS BUILDING

7   We were convinced that the Commonwealth, with its global reach and unique experience of consensus-building, was in a position to assist the wider international community in building bridges across traditional international divides of opinion on particular issues. We therefore agreed that there was scope for the association to play a greater role in the search for consensus on global issues, through:

- use of their governments' membership of various regional organizations and attendance at other international gatherings to advance consensual positions agreed within the Commonwealth;

- use, where appropriate, of special missions to advance Commonwealth consensual positions and promote wider consensus on issues of major international concern; and
- use of formal and informal Commonwealth consultations in the wings of meetings of international institutions with a view to achieving consensus on major concerns.

Source: originally published by the Information and Public Affairs Division (1998)

The Fancourt Commonwealth Declaration on Globalization and People-Centred Development (1999)

In today's world, no country is untouched by the forces of globalization. Our destinies are linked together as never before. The challenge is to seize the opportunities opened up by globalization while minimizing its risks.

On the positive side, globalization is creating unprecedented opportunities for wealth creation and for the betterment of the human condition. Reduced barriers to trade and enhanced capital flows are fuelling economic growth.

The revolution in communications technologies is shrinking the distance between nations, providing new opportunities for the transfer of knowledge and the development of skills-based industries. And, globally, technological advance offers great potential for the eradication of poverty.

But the benefits of globalization are not shared equitably. Prosperity remains the preserve of the few. Despite the progress of the past 50 years, half of the world's population lives on less than US$2 per day. Many millions live in conditions of extreme deprivation. The poor are being marginalized. Expanded capital flows have also brought with them the risk of greater financial instability, undermining the hope that a commitment to open markets can lift the developing world, especially the least developed countries, out of poverty and debt.

The persistence of poverty and human deprivation diminishes us all. It also makes global peace and security fragile, limits the growth of markets and forces millions to migrate in search of a better life. It constitutes a deep and fundamental structural flaw in the world economy.

The greatest challenge, therefore, facing us today is how to channel the forces of globalization in order to eliminate poverty and empower human beings to lead fulfilling lives.

The solution does not lie in abandoning a commitment to market principles or in wishing away the powerful forces of technological change. Globalization is a reality and can only increase in its impact. But if the benefits of globalization are to be shared more widely, there must be greater equity for countries in global markets.

We call on all nations fully to implement the Uruguay Round [of GATT] commitments to dismantle barriers to trade for the mutual benefit of all. Moreover, recognizing, in particular, the significant contribution that enhanced export opportunities can make to reduce poverty, we call for improved market access for the exports of all countries, particularly developing countries, and the removal of all barriers to the exports of the least developed countries.

Strong export growth remains a key element in the ability of developing countries to improve their living standards to the levels enjoyed in the industrialized world. We support efforts that would enable developing countries to build up their skills and manufacturing capacities, including the production and export of value-added goods, in order to enhance growth and achieve prosperity.

Likewise, we urge that the forthcoming Ministerial Meeting of the World Trade Organization (WTO) [Seattle, November 1999] launch the next round of global negotiations on trade with a pronounced developmental dimension, and with the aim of achieving better market access in agriculture, industrial products and services in a way that provides benefits to all members, particularly developing countries. The round should be balanced in process, content and outcome.

We fully believe in the importance of upholding labour standards and protecting the environment. But these must be addressed in an appropriate way that does not, by linking them to trade liberalization, end up impeding free trade and causing injustice to developing countries.

We also call on the global community to establish innovative mechanisms to promote capital flows to a wider number of countries, and to urgently initiate the reform of international financial architecture to minimize financial instability and its impact on the poor.

We believe that the elimination of poverty is achievable – but only if we take determined and concerted action at national and international levels. We reiterate our commitment to work for a reversal of the decline in official development-assistance flows. Urgent action is also required to tackle the unsustainable debt burden of developing countries, particularly the poorest, building on the recent initiatives agreed internationally. We believe such development assistance must be focused on human development, poverty reduction and on the development of capacities for participating in expanding world markets that trade in goods and capital. Above all, we recognize the responsibilities of national governments to promote 'pro-poor' policies and human development.

If the poor and the vulnerable are to be at the centre of development, the process must be participatory so that people have a voice. We believe that the spread of democratic freedoms and good governance, as well as access to education, training and health care, are key to expanding human capabilities and to banishing ignorance and prejudice. Recognizing that good governance and economic progress are directly linked, we affirm our commitment to the pursuit of greater transparency, accountability, the rule of law and the elimination of corruption in all spheres of public life and in the private sector.

We are concerned about the vast gap between the rich and poor in the ability to access new technologies; the concentration of the world's research resources in market-driven products and processes; the increasing tendency to claim proprietary rights on traditional knowledge; and bio-piracy. We call on the world community to use the opportunities offered by globalization to adopt practical measures for overcoming these challenges – for example, by extending the benefits of global medical research through the provision of drugs at affordable prices to the poor in developing countries.

We welcome the spread of ideas, information and knowledge in building civil support for social equality, and in opposing all forms of discrimination and other injustices based on ethnicity, gender, race and religion. However, while better communications have increased human contact, there is for some a growing sense of social exclusion and a general failure of moral purpose. Persistence of inequalities faced by women, continued high levels of youth unemployment, lack of adequate support systems for the aged, children and the disabled in many parts of the world, and increased threats to the diversity of cultures and beliefs all contribute to the undermining of a just and stable society. We therefore call for a renewed commitment to eliminate all forms of discrimination and to take measures that promote respect for the diverse languages, cultures and beliefs, and traditions of the world, which enrich all of our lives.

Recognizing that taking full advantage of the opportunities for development that are created by globalization is not possible without security, political stability and peace, we commit ourselves, in partnership with civil society, to promote processes that help to prevent or resolve conflicts in a peaceful manner, and we support measures that help to stabilize post-conflict situations, as well as combat terrorism of all kinds.

Good governance requires inclusive and participatory processes at both national and international levels. We call on the global community to search for inclusive processes of multilateralism which give a more effective voice to developing countries in the operations of international institutions, and which recognize the particular vulnerabilities of small states.

We believe that the Commonwealth – an association of diverse sovereign nations which reflects different stages of development and is united by common values – has a vital role to play in promoting consensus at national and international levels and in providing practical assistance for creating the capacities needed to promote people-centred development. At the threshold of a new millennium, we look to the Commonwealth, and its family of organizations, to contribute significantly to making the above aspirations a reality.

Fancourt, South Africa
14 November 1999

Notes

CHAPTER 1 THE GOOD SOCIETY IN A GLOBAL CONTEXT

1   According to Nowell-Smith (1954), the earliest recorded reference to the idea of a good society was in ancient Egypt. The term used for a good society was *Ma'at*. This term had three overlapping meanings: being straight, level or even; having order, conformity and regularity; and possessing truth, justice and righteousness.

2   The World Bank's *World Development Reports* from 1990–2000 are a good source of material on how this consensus is articulated in practice, and they provide advice to governments across the world.

3   Edwards (1999) explores these matters in some depth, and quotes Inge Kaul, director of a United Nations think tank charged with finding out how to implement sustainable development, who concluded: 'We simply do not know.'

CHAPTER 2 CIVIL SOCIETY AND PARTICIPATORY RESEARCH

1   Phenomenology has its origins in the work of Edmund Husserl and Martin Heidegger. See Spiegelberg (1982).

2   For technical reasons, statistical reasons assume the null hypothesis, which depending upon the data may (or may not) be rejected at various conventional levels of significance ($p < .05$, or $p < .01$, etc).

3   Capra (1982) summarizes the fall of the mechanistic view of the universe in which conventional science played a big part. The 'new physics' is explained in terms easy for non-scientists to understand. A

more recent development has been 'fuzzy logic', described by Kosko (1993), and the revival of Bayesianism in statistics in which conventional 95 per cent confidence levels (p < .05) are replaced with subjective yardsticks (*The Economist*, 2000).

4   Chambers (1997) cites Gerry Gill, who cites a mathematician who said: 'OK, the data's lousy but it's all we've got.'

CHAPTER 4 FRIENDS AND ENEMIES OF A GOOD SOCIETY

1   Drawn from *Proof in Print*, a publication chronicling rape, defilement and domestic violence cases in Uganda's printed media. *Proof in Print* is a publication of the Media Women's Association, Uganda (1998).

CHAPTER 5 GOOD GOVERNANCE

1   Nyerere (1998) says: 'Our states are so weak and anaemic already that it would almost amount to a crime to weaken them further... Incidentally the world has changed indeed, the withering of the state used to be the ultimate objective of good Marxists. Today the weakening of the state is the immediate objective of free marketers!' Nyerere goes on to explain that a strong state does not mean a blotted state. Rather, in 'a market economy with its laws of the jungle, we need a state that has got the capacity to intervene on behalf of the weak'.

2   Narayan (2000) points out that, while informal associations and networks may help the poor to survive, they serve a 'defensive' and usually not a 'transformative' function. That is, they do little to move the poor out of poverty.

3   Following the riots in Jamaica which were triggered by an increase in the tax on petrol, the prime minister established a committee led by the president of the Private Sector Organization of Jamaica, Peter Moses, and comprising representatives of various other sectors, including NGOs, to review the situation.

References

Abeysekera, C and Weerakoon, B (1996) *Civil Society in Sri Lanka*, International Centre for Ethnic Studies, Colombo

Agere, S (2000) *Promoting Good Governance: Principles, practices and perspectives*, Commonwealth Secretariat, London

Andreski, S (1972) *Social Sciences as Sorcery*, Andre Deutsch, London

Andrusz, G (1999) *The Cooperative Alternative in Europe: The case of housing*, Ashgate, Aldershot

Annan, K (1999) First Diana, Princess of Wales, Memorial Lecture on AIDS, 25 June

Annan, K (1998) 'The quiet revolution', *Global Governance*, vol 4, pp 123–138

Anyang Nyongo, P (1983) *The Economic Foundation of the State in Contemporary Africa: Stratification and social classes*, Presence Africaine, Paris

Arblaster, A and Lukes, S (eds) (1971) *The Good Society*, University Paperbacks, Methuen, London

Argyle, M (1987) *The Psychology of Happiness*, Oxford University Press, Oxford

Arnstein, S (1969) 'A ladder of citizen participation', *Journal of the American Planning Association*, vol 35, no 4, pp216–224

Arthur, C (1999) 'Shares soar in Freeserve stampede', *The Independent*, p2, 27 July

Ascherson, N (1997) 'When Soros debunks capitalism, you know a sea change is on the way', *Independent on Sunday*, p3, 2 February

Ayer, A (1937) *Language, Truth and Logic*, Victor Gollancz, London

Bagkikian, B (1992) *The Media Monopoly*, Beacon Press, Boston

Ball, C and Dunn, L (1995) *Non-Governmental Organizations: Guidelines for good policy and practice*, Commonwealth Foundation, London

Ball, C and Knight, B (1988) *Social Policy and Practice: The need for action*, Centre for Research and Innovation in Social Policy and Practice, London

Batten, T (1962) *Training for Community Development*, Oxford University Press, London

Baun, M (1996) *An Imperfect Union*, Westview Press, Oxford

Bell, M (1995) *In Harm's Way: Reflections of a war zone thug*, Hamish Hamilton, London

Beveridge, W (1948) *Voluntary Action*, Allen and Unwin, London

Bhargave, N and Bhat, M (eds) (2000) *Building Civil Society*, Civil Society Collective, Bangalore

Booth, M (1998) *Opium: A history*, St Martin's Press, New York

Bourdieu, P and Wacquant, L (1992) *Invitation to Reflexive Sociology*, University of Chicago Press, Chicago

Bowlby, J (1946) 'Psychology and democracy', *The Political Quarterly*, vol XVII, pp61–76

Bowlby, J (1956) 'The effects of mother-child separation: a follow-up study', *British Journal of Medical Psychology*, vol 29, pp211–247

Bulmer, M (1986) *Neighbours: The work of Philip Abrams*, Cambridge University Press, Cambridge

Burke, E (1790) *Reflections on the Revolution in France*, Dent (1910), London

Capra, F (1982) *The Turning Point: Science, society and the rising culture*, Wildwood House, London

Central Intelligence Agency (CIA) (2000) *Global Trends 2015: A dialogue about the future with nongovernment experts*, CIA, Washington, DC

Chambers, R (1997) *Whose Reality Counts? Putting the first last*, Intermediate Technology Publications, London

Chigudu, H (2000) 'Africa', unpublished paper, Harare

Christian Science Monitor (1995) 'Wireless Phones Ring Off the Wall', vol 1, issue 7, 31 May

CIVICUS (1999) *Civil Society at the Millennium*, Kumarian Press, West Hartford, Connecticut

CIVICUS Africa Regional Assembly (1999) 'Civil society and the eradication of poverty in Africa', *Report of Proceedings at Kenya College of Communications*, 15–17 June 1999

Cohen, J and Arato, A (1992) *Civil Society and Political Theory*, MIT Press, Cambridge, Massachusetts

Colas, D (1997) *Civil Society and Fanaticism*, Stanford University Press, Stanford

Coleman, J (1990) *Foundations of Social Theory*, Harvard University Press, Cambridge

Convergence (1975) vol 2, no 2

Cornia, G, Jolly, R and Stewart, F (eds) (1996) *Adjustment with a Human Face* (2 volumes), Oxford University Press, Oxford

Cornwall, A and Gaventa, J (2001) 'Bridging the gap: citizen, partnership and accountability', *PLA Notes*, February

Cornwall, A, Guijt, I and Welbourn, A (1994) 'Acknowledging Process: Challenges for agricultural research and extension methodology' in Ian Scoones and John Thompson (eds) *Beyond Farmer First: Rural people's knowledge*, Intermediate Technology Publications, London

Crosland, A (1955) *The Future of Socialism*, Cape (abridged and revised edition, 1965), London

D'Olivera, M and Tandon, R (1995) *Strengthening Global Civil Society*, CIVICUS, Washington, DC

Dahl, R and Tufts, E (1973) *Size and Democracy*, Stanford University Press, Stanford

Dahrendorf, R (1997) 'After 1989' in *Morals, Revolution and Civil Society*, Macmillan, Basingstoke

Davenport, E and Low, W (1999) *Partners in a Common Future: Development for poverty eradication*, Council for International Development, Wellington

de Tocqueville, Alexis (1988) *Democracy in America*, edited by J P Mayer, translated by George Lawrence, Harper and Row, New York

Dietrich, G (1989) *Culture, Religion and Development*, Centre for Social Action, Delhi

Diokno, M (ed) (1997) *Democracy and Citizenship in Filipino Political Culture*, University of the Philippines, Quezon City

Drage, J (1994) 'Women's Representation in the Pacific Islands' in Busch, Crocombe and Ors (eds) *New Politics in the South Pacific*, Institute of Pacific Studies, University of the South Pacific, Suva/Rarotonga

Drucker, P (1997) 'The global economy and the nation-state', *Foreign Affairs*, September–October

Dublin, E (1949) *Problems of Economic Planning*, Routledge, London

Durkheim, E (1893) *The Division of Labour in Society*, Free Press, New York (republished 1933)

Eberly, D (2000) *The Essential Civil Society Reader*, Rowman and Littlefield, Oxford

Edwards, M (1999) *Future Positive: International co-operation in the 21st century*, Earthscan, London

Edwards, M (2000) *NGO Rights and Responsibilities: A new deal for global governance*, Foreign Policy Studies Centre and NCVO, London

Etzioni, A (1995) *The Spirit of Community: Rights, responsibilities and the communitarian agenda*, Fontana, London

Fernandes, K and Fernandes, N (eds) (1997) *How Communities Organize Themselves*, City Press, Karachi

Fowler, A (1997) *Striking a Balance: A guide to enhancing the effectiveness of non-governmental organizations in international development*, Earthscan, London

Freire, P (1970) *Pedagogy of the Oppressed*, The Seabury Press, New York

Fukuyama, F (1989) 'The End of History?', *The National Interest*, no 16 (summer), pp3–18

Fukuyama, F (1992) *The End of History and the Last Man*, Penguin Books, London

Fukuyama, F (1995) *Trust: The social virtues and the creation of prosperity*, Free Press, London

Garcia-Bonza, J (1980) *Basic-Needs Analytical Bibliography*, OECD Development Centre, Paris

Gellner, E (1994) *Conditions of Liberty: Civil society and its rivals*, Hamish Hamilton, London

Ghosh, P (ed) (1984) *Third World Development: A basic needs approach*, Greenwood Press, Westport, Connecticut

Gibson, T (1997) *The Power in Our Hands: Neighbourhood based world shaking*, Charlbury, Oxfordshire

Giddens, A (1999) 'Keynote Speech Delivered at London School of Economics and Political Science', *Third Sector Third Way Conference*, 7 June

Glaser, B and Strauss, A (1970) *The Discovery of Grounded Theory*, Aldine, New York

Goulet, D (1971) *The Cruel Choice: A new choice in the theory of development*, Athenaeum, New York

Gramsci, A (1971) *Selections from Prison Notebooks of A Gramsci*, Hoare, Q and Smith, G N (eds), International Publishers, New York

Greider, W (1992) *Who Will Tell the People? The betrayal of American democracy*, Simon and Schuster, New York

Gulhati, R and Gulhati, K (1999) *Anatomy of Voluntarism: The case of Madya Pradesh*, Konark Publishers, Delhi

Gurr, T et al (1993) *Minorities at Risk: A global view of ethnopolitical conflicts*, Institute of Peace Press, Washington, DC

Habermas, J (1978) 'Legitimation Problems in the Modern State', in *Communication and the Evolution of Society* (translated by Thomas McCarthy), Beacon Press, Boston

Hague, R, Harrop, M and Breslin, S (1998) *Comparative Government and Politics*, Macmillan, Basingstoke (fourth edition)

Hall, J (ed) (1995) *Civil Society: Theory, history, comparison*, Polity Press, Cambridge

Hancock, G (1989) *Lords of Poverty*, Macmillan, London

Hanifan, L J (1920) *The Community Center*, Silver, Burdette and Co, Boston

Hayek, F von (1988) *The Fatal Conceit: The Errors of socialism; The Collected Works of Friedrich August von Hayek* (edited by W W Bartlett), Routledge, London

Helleiner, E (1994) 'From Bretton Woods to Global Finance: A world turned upside down' in Stubbs, R and Underhill, G (eds) *Political Economy and the Changing Global Order*, McClelland and Stewart, Toronto

Higgins, J (1980) *The Poverty Business: Britain and America*, Basil Blackwell and Martin Robertson, Oxford and London

Hirst, P (1994) *Associative Democracy: new forms of economic and social governance*, The University of Massachusetts Press, Amherst

Hobsbawm, E (1994) *Age of Extremes: The short twentieth century 1914–1991*, Michael Joseph, London

Holloway, R *Civil Society Toolbox*, www.pactworld.org/toolbox.html [last accessed September 2001]

Holm, H and Sorensen, G (1995) 'International Relations Theory in a World of Variation' in Holm, H and Sorensen, G (eds) *Whose World Order? Uneven globalization and the end of the cold war*, Westview, Colorado

Hunt, L (1999) 'Civil Society and the Idea of a Commercial Republic' in Schechter, M (ed) *The Revival of Civil Society: Global and comparative perspectives*, St Martin's Press, New York

Huntingdon, S (1996) *The Clash of Civilizations and the Making of World Order*, Simon and Schuster, New York

Ignatieff, M (1999) 'The ascent of man', *Prospect*, October

Indian Social Institute (1997) *Fifty Years After Freedom: New opportunities for voluntary action in India*, Indian Social Institute, New Delhi

International Conference on Popular Participation in the Recovery and Development Process in Africa, (1990) *African Charter for Popular Participation in Development and Transformation*, Arusha

International Labour Organization (ILO) (1976) *Employment, Growth and Basic Needs*, ILO, Geneva

Kapen, S (1994) *Tradition, Modernity and Counterculture: An Asian perspective*, Visthar, Bangalore

Kaplan, R (1994) 'The coming anarchy', *Atlantic Monthly* 273, February, pp44–76

Kassam, Y and Kemal, M (eds) (1982) *Participatory research: an emerging alternative methodology in social science research*, Society for Participatory Research in Asia, Delhi

Kelly, G (1955) *The Psychology of Personal Constructs* (2 volumes), Norton, New York

Keynes, J M (1936) *The General Theory of Employment, Interest and Money*, Macmillan, London (republished in 1961)

Knight, B (1999) 'Community Politics' in Campbell, D and Lewis, N (eds) *Promoting Participation: Law or politics*, Cavendish Publishing, London

Knight, B (1999) 'Towards a perfect civil society', *Alliance*, vol 4, no 2, pp27–39

Knight, B and Hartnell, C (2000) 'Civil society – is it anything more than a metaphor for hope for a better world?' *Alliance*, vol 5, no 3, pp16–18

Knight, B and Stokes, P (1996) *The Deficit in Civil Society in the United Kingdom*, Foundation for Civil Society, Birmingham

Korten, D (1995) *When Corporations Rule the World*, Kumarian Press, West Hartford and Berrett-Koehler, San Francisco

Kosko, B (1993) *Fuzzy Thinking: The new science of fuzzy logic*, Harper Collins, London

Kramer, S and Roberts, J (1996) *The Politics of Attachment: Towards a secure society*, Free Association Books, London

Kuenstler, P (1960) *New Community Organization*, Faber and Faber, London

Kumar, K (1993) 'Civil Society: An inquiry into the usefulness of an historical term', *The British Journal of Sociology*, vol 44, no 3, pp375–389

Landry, C and Mulgan, G (1995) *The Other Invisible Hand: remaking charity for the 21st century*, Demos, London

Lenin, V (1917) 'State and revolution' in *Selected Works*, Lawrence and Wishart, London (republished in 1969)

Leys, C (1996), *The Rise and Fall of Development Theory*, James Currey, Oxford

Lisk, F (1983) 'Conventional Development Strategies and Basic Needs Fulfilment' in Todaro, M (ed) *The Struggle for Economic Development: Readings in problems and policies*, Longman, New York

Malik, Iftikhar H (1997) *State and Civil Society in Pakistan: Politics of authority, ideology and ethnicity*, Macmillan, London

Mammoon, M and Ray, J (1998) *Civil Society in Bangladesh: Resilience and retreat*, Ahmed Mahfuzul Haq, Dhaka

Marshall, R (1995) 'The global jobs crisis', *Foreign Policy* (Fall), pp50–68

Mayo, M (1975) 'Community Development: A radical alternative?' in Bailey, R and Brake, M (eds) *Radical Social Work*, Edward Arnold, London

Mbogori, E and Chigudu, H (1999) 'Civil Society and Government: A continuum of possibilities' in CIVICUS, *Civil Society at the Millennium*, Kumarian Press, West Hartford, Connecticut

McCarthy, K, Hodgkinson, V et al (1991) (eds) *Nonprofit Sector in the Global Community: Voices from many nations*, Independent Sector, Washington, DC

McLuhan, M (1962) *The Gutenberg Galaxy*, University of Toronto Press, Toronto

Michels, R (1911) *Political Parties* (translated by Paul, E and Paul, C) Dover Publications, New York (republished in 1959)

Midgely, J (1986) *Community Participation, Social Development and the State*, Methuen, London

Mill, J S (1948) *Principles of Political Economy*, Longman, London (originally published in 1848)

Ministry of Finance (1999) *Planning and Economic Development: Participatory poverty assessment, poor people's perspective*, Government of Uganda, Kampala

Mowlana, H (1995) 'The communications paradox', *Bulletin of the Atomic Scientists*, vol 51 (July), pp42–44

Mutunga, W (1999) *Constitution Making from the Middle: Civil society and transition politics in Kenya 1992–1997*, MWENGO, Harare

Myers, S (ed) (1999) *Democracy Is a Discussion II*, Connecticut College, New London, Connecticut

Nagaraja, B and Bhat, M (eds) (2000) *Building Civil Society: Bangalore,* India Civil Society Collective, Delhi

Naidoo, K (2000) 'Perspectives on civil society: its relation to third sector research', *International Society of Third Sector Research Conference,* 5–8 July, Dublin

Narayan, D (2000) *Voices of the Poor: Can anyone hear us?,* Oxford University Press for the World Bank, New York

Narayan, D, Chambers, R, Shah, M and Petesch, P D (2000) *Crying out for Change,* World Bank, New York

Norman, P (2001) 'A sense of disconnecton', *Financial Times,* 18 June

Norris, P (1999) *Critical Citizens,* Oxford University Press, Oxford

Nowell-Smith, P (1954) *Ethics,* Penguin, Harmondsworth

Nyang'oro, J (ed) (1999) *Civil Society and Democracy in Eastern and Southern Africa,* MWENGO, Harare

Nyerere, J (1998) *Governance in Africa,* SAPEM, Harare

Oakeshott, M (1956) 'On being conservative', in Oakeshott, M, *Rationalism in Politics,* Methuen, London (republished in 1962)

Overseas Development Agency (ODA) (1993) cited by Hulme and Turner (1997) *Governance, Administration and Development: Making the state work,* Macmillan Press, Basingstoke

Organization for Economic Cooperation and Development (OECD) (1993) *Participatory Development and Good Governance,* OECD, Paris

OECD (1994) *Development Cooperation, Efforts and Policies of the Members of the Development Assistance Committee,* 1993 Report, OECD, Paris

Olin, A (1995) *Civil Society in Transition: Local level associational life in Zambia,* SIDA, Stockholm

Otterbein, K (1990) 'Two styles of cross-cultural research', *CAM (Cultural Anthropology Methods) Newsletter,* vol 2, issue 3, pp3–7, November

Palan, R and Abbott, J (1996) *State Strategies in the Global Economy,* Pinter, London

Pandey, G (1993) 'Rallying round the Cow: Sectarian strife in the Bhojpuri region, c. 1888–1917' in Ranajit, G (ed) *Subaltern Studies 2: Writings on South Asian history and society,* Oxford University Press, Delhi

Pateman, C (1970) *Participation and Democratic Theory,* Cambridge University Press, Cambridge

Pearl, A and Reissman, F (eds) (1965) *New Careers for the Poor,* Free Press, New York

Pew Charitable Trusts (1998) www.puaf.umd.edu/civicrenewal

Puthucheary, M (1998) *The Politics of Administration,* Oxford University Press, Kuala Lumpur
Putnam, R (1993) *Making Democracy Work: Civic traditions in modern Italy*, Princeton University Press, Princeton
Putnam, R (1993) *Making Democracy Work: Civic Traditions in Modern Italy*, Princeton University Press, New Jersey
Putnam R (1995) 'Bowling Alone: America's declining social capital', *Journal of Democracy,* vol 6, no 1
Putnam, R (1995) 'Bowling alone, revisited', *The Responsive Community*, spring
Putnam, R (2000) *Bowling Alone*, Simon and Schuster, New York
Raffer, K and Singer, H (1996) *The Foreign Aid Business: Economic assistance and development cooperation*, Edward Elgar, Aldershot
Rozen, L (1999) 'Organised gangs rule Kosovo', *The Independent*, p14, 3 August
Sachs, W (ed) (1992) *The Development Dictionary: A guide to knowledge as power*, Zed Books, London and New Jersey
Salamon, L (1994) 'The Rise of the Nonprofit Sector', *Foreign Affairs*, vol 74 no 3, July/August
Salamon, L and Anheier, H (1994) *The Emerging Sector: an overview*, The Johns Hopkins Comparative Nonprofit Sector Project Studies, Baltimore
Salamon, L, Anheier, H, List, R, Toepler, S, Wojciech Sokolowski, S et al (1999*) Global Civil Society: Dimensions of the nonprofit sector*, Johns Hopkins Centre for Civil Society Studies, Baltimore
SARRC (1992) *Meeting the Challenge*, SARRC, Kathmandu
Schechter, M (ed) (1999) *The Revival of Civil Society: global and comparative perspectives*, St Martin's Press, New York
Schumpeter, J (1942) *Capitalism, Socialism and Democracy*, Allen and Unwin, London
Selbourne, D (1994) *The Principle of Duty: An essay on the foundations of the civic order,* Sinclair-Stevenson, London
Seligman, A (1992) *The Idea of Civil Society*, Princeton University Press, Princeton
Serrano, I (1994) *Civil Society in the Asia Pacific Region*, CIVICUS, Washington, DC
Serrano, I (1999) 'Dealing with normative conflicts' in Anhelm (ed) *Stiftungen und NGOs als Architekten des Wandels*, Loccumer Protokolle, Loccum

Sherma, C (1990) *A Look Inside the World Bank*, Envirobook, Sydney

Smillie, I (1995) *The Alms Bazaar: Altruism Under Fire – Non-profit organizations and international development*, Intermediate Technology Publications, London

Smith, A (1776) *An Inquiry into the Nature and Causes of the Wealth of Nations*, 2 volumes, W Strahan and T Cadell, London

SPEAR (1997) 'Project for democracy, an advocacy case study' in SPEAR, *Belize National Report*, Commonwealth Foundation, Belize

Spiegelberg, H (1982) *The Phenomenological Movement* (third edition), Martinus Nijhoff, The Hague

Stern, R (1993) *Changing India*, Cambridge University Press, Cambridge

Stewart, A (1969) 'The Social Roots' in Ionescu, G and Gellner, E (eds) *Populism: Its meanings and national characteristics*, Macmillan, New York

Stiefel, M and Wolfe, M (1994) *A Voice for the excluded, Popular participation in development: utopia or necessity?*, Zed Books Limited in association with the UNRISD, London

Strange, S (1995) 'The Limits of Politics', *Text of the Government and Opposition Leonard Schapiro Lecture*, delivered at the London School of Economics and Political Science, 1 June

Streeten, P (1993) 'From Growth Via Basic Needs, to Human Development: The Individual in the process of development' in Murshed, S and Raffer, K (eds) *Trade, Transfers and Development: Problems and Prospects for the Twenty-First Century*, Edward Elgar, Aldershot

Sturgess, Gary (1996) 'The boundaries of life's responsibilities: community and nation in a global environment', *CIS Occasional Paper 57*, Centre for Independent Studies

Sutherland, E and Cressey, D (1970) *Criminology* (eighth edition), Lippincott, New York

Tadashi, Y (ed) (1999) *Deciding the Public Good: Governance and civil society in Japan*, Japan Centre for International Exchange, Tokyo

Tandon, R (1986) 'Knowledge as Power: Participatory research as alternative' in Fernandes, W (ed) *Dr Alfred De Souza Memorial Essays*, Indian Social Institute, Delhi

Tandon, R (1997) 'Struggle for knowledge: a personal journey', *Paper given at Fourth World Congress on Action Research*, Colombia, South America, 1–5 June

Tandon, R (1997) 'Civil society and construction of knowledge systems', *Paper given at Fourth World Congress on Action Research*, Colombia, South America, 1–5 June

Tandon, R (2000) 'Citizens and governance: the challenge of civil society in the new millennium', *International Society for Third Sector Research Conference Paper*, Dublin, 5–8 July

Tandon, Y (1997) 'An Economic Agenda for the Left', *The Journal of Social Change,* no 48, p9

Taylor, C (1995) *Invoking Civil Society: Philosophical arguments*, Harvard University Press, Cambridge, Massachusetts

The Economist (1997) 'Not Quite a New World Order: More a three way split', 20 December

The Economist (1998) 'World Trade Survey', 3 October

The Economist (1999) 'Exporting Misery', 17 April

The Economist (1999) 'Work in Progress', 24 July

The Economist (2000) 'In Praise of Bayesianism' 4 October

Thornton, P (1999) 'World jitters are set to hit fever pitch', *The Independent*, p18, 2 August

Titmuss, R (1970) *The Gift Relationship*, Allen and Unwin, London

Todaro, M (1991) *Economic Development in the Third World*, Orient Longman, Hyderabad

Tuckman, B W (1965) 'Interpersonal probing and revealing and systems of integrative complexity', *Journal of Personal and Social Psychology*, vol 3, pp655–664

Turner, J (1976) *Housing by People: Towards autonomy in building environments*, Marion Boyars, London and New York

United Nations Development Programme (UNDP) (1997) *Management Development and Governance*, Division Bureau for Policy and Programme Support Unit, UNDP, April

United Nations (1998) *Human Development Report*, UN, Washington, DC

US Census Bureau Estimate (1999) 'Populous Planet Passes 6 Billion', reported by Linus Gregoriadis, *The Independent*, p17, 19 July

US Government Commerce Department (1999) *The Emerging Digital Economy II*, US Government Commerce Department, Washington, DC

Van Creveld, M (1991) *On Future War*, The Free Press, London

Van Rooy, A and Robinson, M (1998) 'Out of the ivory tower: civil society and the aid system' in Van Rooy, A (ed) *Civil Society and the Aid Industry*, Earthscan, London

Vidal, J (1997) 'Environment: The real politics of power', *The Guardian*, 'Society' section, p4, 30 April

Waddington, C (1977) *Tools for Thought*, Jonathan Cape, London

Waldren, M (1999) *Future Tense: Australian beyond election 1998*, Allen & Unwin, Sydney

Wann, M (1995) *Building Social Capital: Self help in a twenty-first state*, Institute for Public Policy Research, London

Watkins, K (1995) *The Oxfam Poverty Report*, Oxfam, Oxford

Wignaraja, P and Hussein, A (1989) 'The Crisis and Promise in South Asia' in Wignaraja, P and Hussein, A (eds) *The Challenge in South Asia: Development, democracy, and regional cooperation*, Sage Publications India, Delhi

Wilde, O (1891) 'The Soul of Man Under Socialism' in *Selected Essays and Poems*, Penguin, London (republished in 1954)

Wiles, P (1969) 'A Syndrome, Not a Doctrine' in Ionescu, G and Gellner, E (eds) *Populism: Its meanings and national characteristics*, Macmillan, New York

Wilks, A (2000) 'Poor relations', *Third Sector*, vol 198, p17, 14 December

Winnicott, D (1964) *The Child, the Family and the Outside World*, Penguin, London

'Wireless Phones Ring Off the Wall' (1995) *Christian Science Monitor*, vol 1, p7, 31 May

World Bank (1992) *Governance and Development*, World Bank, Washington, DC

World Bank (1990) Cooperation between the World Bank and NGOs, *Progress Report*, Washington, DC, 8 March

World Bank (1991) *The Challenge of Development: World Bank Development Report*, Oxford University Press, New York

World Bank (1994) *Governance: The World Bank's experience*, World Bank, Washington, DC

World Bank (1996) *From Plan to Market: World Bank Development Report*, Oxford University Press, New York

World Bank (1997) *The State in a Changing World: World Bank Development Report*, Oxford University Press, New York

World Bank (1999) *Entering the 21st Century: The World Bank Development Report 1999/2000*, Oxford University Press, New York

World Bank (2000) *Attacking Poverty: World Bank Development Report*, New York: Oxford University Press, New York

Wright, R (2000) 'Global Happiness', *Prospect*, December, pp34–38

Yamamoto, T (ed) (1995) *Emerging Civil Society in the Asia Pacific*, Community Institute for South-East Asian Studies, Singapore

Index

Significant information in notes is indexed in the form 191n3(1), ie page 191, note 3 of Chapter 1